Philip Larkin: A Bibliography

Photo: Rollie McKenna

Philip Larkin, 1960

Philip Larkin

A BIBLIOGRAPHY

1933–1976

by
B. C. BLOOMFIELD

FABER AND FABER
London · Boston

First published in 1979
by Faber and Faber Limited
3 Queen Square London WC1N 3AU
Printed in Great Britain by
Western Printing Services, Bristol
All rights reserved

British Library Cataloguing in Publication Data

Bloomfield, Barry Cambray
Philip Larkin.
1. Larkin, Philip – Bibliography
016.821'9'14   Z8483./

ISBN 0–571–11447–4

CONTENTS

	Introduction	*page* 9
	Foreword	11
	Acknowledgements	13
	Abbreviations	15
A.	Books and Pamphlets by Philip Larkin	17
B.	Works edited or with contributions by Philip Larkin	59
C.	Contributions by Philip Larkin to periodicals	77
D.	Larkin at the University of Hull	107
E.	Interviews	117
F.	Recordings	121
G.	Radio and television appearances	127
H.	Odds and ends	131
I.	Manuscripts	137
J.	Published letters	141
K.	Translations	145
L.	Anthologies	151
	Appendix	
	Bibliography and criticism of Larkin's work	157
	Index	167

INTRODUCTION

'There'll be books . . . ' (*Going, going*)

I embarked on this bibliography because I receive much pleasure from reading Philip Larkin's poems; but I also experienced great difficulty in finding out more about the poems, especially the circumstances of their original publication. Having met Dr Larkin at some of the numerous conferences librarians organize for their mutual benefit and having, as we do, several tastes in common, my suggestion that I should undertake this listing was somewhat reluctantly agreed.

The result is closely modelled, as bibliographers may recognize, on *W. H. Auden: a Bibliography, 1924–1969* (2nd edn. Charlottesville, University Press of Virginia, 1972) and the aim of this bibliography is to be as practically useful as possible to the student and reader of Philip Larkin's poetry. Section A of the bibliography lists books and pamphlets by Larkin and follows normal bibliographical practice in describing these items except in one particular: what is normally referred to, bibliographically speaking, as the 'Contents note' is subjoined to the collation, while the heading 'Contents' is reserved for the listing of the literary contents of the book being described; *i.e.* the word is used in its generally accepted sense.

Normal practice is observed when transcribing upper- and lower-case letters; italic is used for any of the modern sloping type faces; and coloured printing is indicated in square brackets placed before the relevant words or letters. No differentiation is made between small and large upper-case letters.

The first impression of the first edition is usually fully described, and only where notable differences occur are later impressions included or mentioned. Where corrections to the text are made in subsequent impressions these are usually mentioned. Editions subsequent to the first are described in briefer form.

The colours of binding cloths are described according to the scheme proposed by Professor G. T. Tanselle in 'A system of color identification for bibliographical description' (*Studies in Bibliography*, XX [1967], 203–34). A brief descriptive note has been included for any dust jacket.

Under the heading 'Contents' an attempt has been made, as each poem is listed, to give its previous and subsequent printings. Thus, knowing the first appearance in collected form of any particular piece, one may glean some idea of its textual history.

The listing of reviews is not exhaustive although I hope it includes all those of any importance, while excluding many minor notices. In the notes, in addition to the publishing information, I have tried where possible to give some information about the composition of some items.

Section B follows the plan of the first section except that the collations of the items described are much abbreviated and reviews have been listed only for *The Oxford Book of Twentieth-Century English Verse*. These were included because so many reviewers when discussing the anthology devoted most of their space to the anthologist rather than the published work.

Section C contains Larkin's contributions to periodicals and is arranged in order of date of publication, and section D lists material written by Larkin in the course of his duties as Librarian at the University of Hull. Other sections list Larkin's varied contributions to radio, television, etc., and recordings of his poetry read by himself. There are problems in describing these contributions to other media and I do not pretend to have solved them. However I hope that by listing them in a fairly detailed fashion I have made the lot of the Larkin critic considerably easier. The bibliography concludes with a listing of Larkin criticism and an index to the whole. The terminal date for all sections is December 1976.

I shall be very glad to receive corrections, additions and amplifications for the improvement of the bibliography and they should be sent to me care of the publisher.

B. C. BLOOMFIELD
(alias J.B.)

February 1977

FOREWORD

When Mr Bloomfield wrote to me in 1972 to say that, having finished the second edition of his Auden bibliography, he was 'casting around for a fresh victim', I was naturally honoured. The science of bibliography, with its cancels and chipped e's, has never greatly appealed to me, but Mr. Bloomfield's volumes, relating as they did to a major poet whose work I admired, were immediately fascinating. While scrupulously professional in their approach, they were enriched with original information quarried from neglected sources or even communicated by the poet himself, along with hard facts on printing numbers that in themselves constituted essential material for an economic history of poetry. The thought of having this technique employed upon myself was at once exhilarating and alarming, and I accepted without hesitation.

Some two years passed before Mr Bloomfield paid me a professional visit, but when he did he already possessed a great deal more information than I should have believed possible, making me doubt whether his early admonition that 'complete honesty prevails between bibliographer and bibliographee' was really necessary. Any thoughts I may have had about glossing over certain literary indiscretions were dispelled: Mr Bloomfield's normally friendly and undemanding demeanour now held disquieting overtones of the investigator, the auditor, at times even the Alcoholics Anonymous counsellor or the Oxford Group 'sharer'. Soon I was supplying evidence against myself as eagerly as any Russian state trial defendant. When he left he sent my secretary flowers, a kindly thought that at the time seemed immeasurably sinister.

The interrogation continued over the next eighteen months—not only of myself, but of retired printers dozing in Chelmsford or Redditch; of remote American publishers; of numerous librarians, curators and information officers everywhere; even of the public at large by means of the appropriate column in the *Times Literary Supplement* ('any information about his work, and especially the whereabouts of . . .'). I think it amused Mr Bloomfield to hint that he sat at the centre of a world-wide network of informants (as no doubt he did): 'New

York is being *difficult*,' he would say. 'I must exert a little pressure,' and he would sometimes startle me by quoting some long-hidden embarrassment—my Second XV Football Character, for instance, or the reports I wrote for my first committee. But such teasing would be balanced by long amusing letters, and often a little gift: a thirties book on the cinema containing an essay by Betjeman, or some of Auden's Creweian Orations.

A list of everything one has written arouses conflicting emotions. First of all one feels flattered that such trouble should have been taken, yet apprehensive lest other people should think one thought it worth taking. Then there is the surprise that so much could be dredged up; as someone who has never been anything but a spare-time writer, and so has tended to refuse commissions rather than accept them, I seem to have done a good many none the less. This in turn provokes a realization of how much one would have to write to make a living by it, and also of the paradox that one can in fact reach the stage of being bibliographized without ever having looked like making a living by it. I suppose most spare-time writers sometimes speculate on whether, if they had always sat down to write after breakfast instead of after supper, what they wrote would have been substantially different. But probably the most lasting reflection is that looking back at one's work is rather like looking back at one's life: it has not really turned out as one intended, little of it is worth mentioning, and much remains that will now never be done. On the other hand, I have, on balance, been lucky, not least in engaging Mr Bloomfield's attention, and for this I am grateful, even if the result is another monument to his own industry and knowledge as much as to any achievement of mine.

PHILIP LARKIN

1978

ACKNOWLEDGEMENTS

I am grateful for and pleased to be able to acknowledge the help and kindnesses I have received from many persons and institutions in the course of compiling this bibliography. My main debt of gratitude is to Dr Philip Larkin himself who put up with my enquiries for the past several years with admirable patience and restraint, and to him I must join Brenda Moon his Deputy, Betty Mackereth his Secretary, and many others on the staff of the University of Hull. Then I wish to acknowledge the help given by Professor C. B. Cox, Dr George Cushing, Mr Peter Ferguson, Mr C. C. Gunner, Professor Edward Mendelson, Mr Alan Plater, Mr T. d'Arch Smith, Mr John Whitehead; and, among my colleagues, by Jonathan Barker, librarian of the Poetry Library, Arts Council; the staff of the British Broadcasting Corporation's Sound Archives and Written Archives Centre; the late F. E. Brazier, librarian of the *Sunday Times*; the staff of the British Institute of Recorded Sound; Miss I. Buchan, formerly of the University of Leicester library; Dennis Cox, librarian of the Brotherton library, University of Leeds; Lynda Farnsworth, Poole library; Mr E. A. Harwood, librarian of the *Daily Telegraph*; Henry Heaney, formerly librarian of Queen's University, Belfast; Mr R. P. Lawrence, librarian of Wellington Branch library; Mr K. L. Mark, literary department of the *Observer*; Roger Mortimer, special collections librarian, Washington University library; Julian Roberts, Bodleian library; Mr F. B. Singleton, librarian of the *Guardian*; and Helen Solley, formerly of Royal Holloway College library.

To these must be added the publishers of Dr Larkin's work who have been very ready with help and information, especially Faber & Faber (Charles Monteith, Brian Dickson and Miranda Pearson-Rogers); Basil Blackwell and Mott; Farrar, Straus & Giroux (Pat Strachan); Farncombe & Co.; George C. Harrap; the Controller of Her Majesty's Stationery Office; S. C. Jennings & Co.; Michael Joseph; Mr J. R. Leach of the Knole Park Press; J. Looker Ltd.; The Marvell Press (George Hartley); The Overlook Press; Oxford University Press, (Catherine Carver); Stiftung F.V.S.; The Villiers Press (John Sankey); Charles Skilton The Fortune Press; and the Yorkshire Arts Association.

I also wish to thank the School of Oriental and African Studies which released me on study leave for three months in the summer of 1974 to allow me to work on this bibliography and another book.

I offer my thanks to those named above and to many others I have bothered with my inquiries in libraries and publishing offices in this country and the United States. I hope they will consider that the result justifies the trouble they took.

B. C. BLOOMFIELD

February 1977

ABBREVIATIONS

Certain of Larkin's books are normally referred to in the bibliography by abbreviations; these are listed below.

NS   *The North Ship*. The Fortune Press, 1945.
        [Second edition.] The Fortune Press, [1965].
        [Third edition.] Faber, 1966.
TLD *The Less Deceived*. The Marvell Press, 1955.
        [American edition.] St. Martin's Press, 1960.
TWW *The Whitsun Weddings*. Faber, 1964.
        [American edition.] Random House, 1964.
AWJ *All What Jazz*. Faber, 1970.
        [American issue.] St. Martin's Press, 1970.
HW   *High Windows*. Faber, 1974.
        [American edition.] Farrar, Straus, Giroux, 1974.

A

BOOKS AND PAMPHLETS
BY
PHILIP LARKIN

A1 THE NORTH SHIP 1945

(a) First edition

THE|NORTH|SHIP|*Poems*|*by*|PHILIP LARKIN|THE FORTUNE
PRESS,|79 Buckingham Palace Road,|LONDON.

Collation: 7⅜× 5 in. [190× 125 mm.] [1–2]⁸[3]⁴, pp. [i–iv, 1–2] 3–35 [36].
[i] 'THE NORTH SHIP'. [ii]: blank. [iii]: title page. [iv]: 'To|S.L. and
E.E.L.|in gratitude'. [1]: contents. [2]: 'FIRST EDITION, 1945|MADE
AND PRINTED IN GREAT BRITAIN'. 3–[36]: text, with last line of p. [36]
reading 'Printed at Redhill by S. C. Jennings & Sons, Ltd.'.

Binding: Bound in smooth black cloth lettered up the spine in gold:
'THE NORTH SHIP—Philip Larkin'. Top edge only trimmed. Deep red
dust jacket printed in black describes this as a volume in 'THE FORTUNE
POETS' series.

Paper: White laid paper watermarked: '*I Batchelor & Sons Ltd*|HAND
MADE'.

Contents:

I All catches alight ... First printed in *Poetry from Oxford in
Wartime*. Dedicated to Bruce Montgomery.

II This was your place of birth, this daytime palace ... First
printed in *Cherwell*, 28 February 1942.

III The moon is full tonight ... First printed in *Poetry from
Oxford in Wartime*.

IV Dawn: To wake, and hear a cock ...

V Conscript: The ego's county he inherited ... First printed in
Phoenix, October–November 1941. Dedicated to James Ballard
Sutton.

VI Kick up the fire, and let the flames break loose ...

VII The horns of the morning ... First printed in *Poetry from
Oxford in Wartime*.

VIII Winter: In the field, two horses ... Reprinted in *Recognitions*,
Winter 1971.

IX Climbing the hill within the deafening wind ...

X Within the dream you said ...

XI Night-music: At one the wind rose ...

XII Like the train's beat ... Reprinted in *Poetry Northwest*, June
1959.

XIII I put my mouth . . . First printed in *Poetry from Oxford in Wartime*.

XIV Nursery tale: All I remember is . . .

XV The dancer: And if she were to admit . . .

XVI The bottle is drunk out one by one . . . First printed in *Poetry from Oxford in Wartime*, and reprinted in *Poetry Northwest*, June 1959.

XVII To write one song, I said . . .

XVIII If grief could burn out . . .

XIX Ugly sister: I will climb thirty steps to my room . . .

XX I see a girl dragged by the wrists . . . First printed in *Poetry from Oxford in Wartime*, and reprinted in *Poetry Northwest*, June 1959.

XXI I dreamed of an out-thrust arm of land . . . First printed in *Arabesque*, Hilary term 1943, and *Oxford poetry, 1942–1943*.

XXII One man walking a deserted platform . . .

XXIII If hands could free you, heart . . .

XXIV Love, we must part now: do not let it be . . . First printed in *Poetry from Oxford in Wartime*.

XXV Morning has spread again . . . First printed in *Poetry from Oxford in Wartime*.

XXVI This is the first thing . . .

XXVII Heaviest of flowers, the head . . . First printed in *Poetry from Oxford in Wartime*.

XXVIII Is it for now or for always . . .

XXIX Pour away that youth . . .

XXX So through that unripe day you bore your head . . . First printed in *Poetry from Oxford in Wartime*. Line 14 misprints 'provincial' as 'provisional'; this is repeated in the second edition.

XXXI The North ship. Legend: I saw three ships go sailing by . . . Songs. 65° N.: My sleep is cold . . . Reprinted in *Poetry Northwest*, June 1959; 70° N.: Fortunetelling: "You will go a long journey . . . 75° N.: Blizzard: Suddenly clouds of snow . . . Above 80° N.: "A woman has ten claws . . .

Notes: Published in July 1945 at 6s. No records have been located for the Fortune Press during this period and the printing offices of S. C. Jennings & Sons have been demolished and their records pulped. However it is not likely that the edition exceeded 500 copies, which were never all sold since the firm of Charles Skilton The Fortune Press inherited "a small packet" of copies of this edition, but without dust jackets, which had been inadvertently destroyed previously. *Whitaker's four year cumulative book list 1944–47* lists the book as published in March 1946; it is not listed in the *English Catalogue of Books*. The best account of the circumstances of the book's publication is given in the author's introduction to the first Faber edition described below.

(b) Second (unauthorized) edition 1965

THE | NORTH | SHIP | *Poems* | *by* | PHILIP LARKIN | THE FORTUNE PRESS | 15 BELGRAVE ROAD, LONDON, S.W.1

Collation: 9⅛ × 5⅝ in. [218 × 144 mm.] [1]⁸[2]⁴[3]⁸, pp. [i–iv, 1–2] 3–35 [36].

[i]: 'THE NORTH SHIP'. [ii]: blank. [iii]: title page. [iv]: 'To | S.L. and E.E.L. | in gratitude'. [1]: contents. [2]: 'FIRST PUBLISHED, 1945 | MADE AND PRINTED IN GREAT BRITAIN'. 3–[36]: text, with the last line on p. [36] reading 'PRINTED AT SEVENOAKS BY KNOLE PARK PRESS LTD.'.

Binding: Bound in smooth dark red (16) buckram lettered up the spine in gold: '*THE NORTH SHIP—Philip Larkin*'. Top and leading edges trimmed. Pale orange dust jacket printed in black.

Paper: White wove unwatermarked paper.

Contents: As the first edition.

Notes: Probably published in April 1965 in an edition of 500 copies at 21s. No records of the Fortune Press during this period have been located and the Knole Park Press Ltd has closed down. However the retired Director, Mr J. R. Leach, was able to trace that 500 copies were invoiced to Mr R. A. Caton for the Fortune Press on 27 February 1965. These sheets would have been delivered to the binders and binding would have taken about six weeks at that time.

The edition was withdrawn from sale when the author discovered its existence and in 1972 the firm of Charles Skilton The Fortune Press still had in stock 220 copies which could not be sold. The copies had no dust jackets as these had inadvertently been destroyed when the stock was transferred.

(c) First Faber edition   1966

THE│NORTH│SHIP│*by*│PHILIP   LARKIN│FABER   AND   FABER│24
Russell Square│London

Collation: 8½× 5½ in. [216× 138 mm.] [A]–C⁸, pp. [1–4] 5–48. [1]: *'The
North Ship'*. [2]: 'By the same author│[twelve lines]'. [3]: title page.
[4]: *'First published in mcmxlv │ First published in this edition mcmlxvi │ by
Faber and Faber Limited │ 24 Russell Square London W C 1 │ Printed in Great
Britain by │ The Bowering Press Plymouth │ All rights reserved │ To │ S.L. and
E.E.L. │ in gratitude │ © 1966 by Philip Larkin'*. 5–6: contents. 7–10:
introduction. 11–48: text.

Binding: Bound in dark purplish-blue (201) cloth lettered down the
spine in gold: 'THE NORTH SHIP Philip Larkin Faber'. Light blue
dust jacket printed in black and bluish grey.

Paper: White wove unwatermarked paper.

Contents: As the first edition but with the addition of a new introduc-
ion and a final poem:—
XXXII   Waiting for breakfast, while she brushed her hair . . . First
        printed in *XX poems* and reprinted in the *Poetry Book Society
        Bulletin*, July 1956.

Notes: Published 15 September 1966 in an impression of 2,500 copies at
15s. and reprinted in December 1967 (2,000 copies). Out of print in
1972.

Reviews: E. Blunden. *Daily Telegraph*, 10 November 1966, p. 20.
        J. Carey. *New Statesman*, LXXIII (30 September 1966), 482.
        E. Jennings. *Spectator*, CCXVII (23 September 1966), 385–6.
        J. Press. *Punch*, CCLI (7 December 1966), 867.
        C. Ricks. *Sunday Times*, 25 September 1966, p. 28.
        M. Seymour-Smith. *Scotsman* [week-end magazine], 8
        October 1966, p. 3.
        Times Educational Supplement, 2 December 1966, p. 1380.
        Times Literary Supplement, 6 October 1966, p. 916.

(d) First paperback impression   1973

THE│NORTH│SHIP│*by*│PHILIP LARKIN│FABER AND FABER│3 Queen
Square│London

Collation: 7¾× 5 in. [197× 129 mm.] [A]–C⁸, pp. [1–4] 5–48. [1]: *'The*

North Ship'. [2]: 'by the same author | [eight lines]'. [3]: title page. [4]:
'*First published in 1945 | First published in cased edition 1966 | First pub-*
lished in this edition 1973 | by Faber and Faber Limited | 3 Queen Square
London W C 1 | Printed in Great Britain by | Whitstable Litho Straker
Brothers Ltd. | All rights reserved | ISBN 0 571 10503 3 (paper covers) | To |
S.L. and E.E.L. | in gratitude | © *1966 by Philip Larkin*'. 5–6: contents.
7–10: introduction. 11–48: text.

Binding: Glued in a very pale-blue (184) paper cover lettered down the
spine: '[in black] PHILIP LARKIN [in greyish blue (186)] THE NORTH
SHIP Faber'; and across the front cover: '[in greyish blue] PHILIP |
[in black] LARKIN | [greyish-blue stripe above a black stripe] | [greyish
blue] THE | [black] NORTH | [greyish blue] SHIP | [black stripe above a
greyish-blue stripe]'. The rear cover carries a list of poets published by
Faber and Faber.

The second impression of this paperback issue is glued in a white,
shiny card cover printed in light blue (181), greyish blue and black.

Paper: White wove unwatermarked paper.

Contents: As the first Faber edition.

Notes: Published in November 1973 in an impression of 3,000 copies
at 95p, and reprinted in April 1974 (5,000 copies).

A2   JILL   1946

(a) First edition

JILL | *by* | PHILIP LARKIN | THE FORTUNE PRESS | London, S. W. 1

Collation: 7¼ × 5 in. [183 × 120 mm.] [π]⁴A–F¹⁶, pp. [1–7] 8–200.
[1]: 'JILL'. [2]: 'Also by PHILIP LARKIN: | THE NORTH SHIP (Poems)'.
[3]: title page. [4]: 'FIRST PUBLISHED IN 1946 | MADE AND PRINTED
IN GREAT BRITAIN'. [5]: author's note. [6]: 'To | JAMES BALLARD
SUTTON'. [7]–200: text, with last line on p. 200 reading '*Printed at*
Lewes by Farncombe & Co. (1928) Ltd.'.

Binding: Bound in dark-blue (183) buckram lettered across the spine in
gold: 'JILL | PHILIP | LARKIN | THE | FORTUNE | PRESS'. Top edge
only cut and sprinkled brown; yellow dust jacket printed in red.

It was the practice of Mr R. A. Caton, the owner of the Fortune Press at that time, to bind up small quantities of any one title at a time using binding cloths which he had acquired cheaply. There appears to be no way of assigning priority to any of these bindings. However, the following variants have been seen:— 1, smooth black cloth with all edges trimmed and top edge sprinkled brown; 2, light-brown (57) cloth with all edges trimmed and top edge sprinkled reddish brown, dust jacket light orange yellow; 3, light yellowish grey (93) cloth with all edges trimmed; and 4, dark reddish-brown (44) shiny bubbled cloth with all edges trimmed and top edge sprinkled brown. (Bloomfield's copy of this last issue has the first gathering wrongly folded and bound so as to page 3, 4, 1, 2, 7, 8, 5 and 6.) What seems to be the latest issue is bound in black Linson patterned paper boards and the dust jacket carries the price 12s. 6d.

Paper: White laid paper watermarked: '[crown] | Glastonbury', using a long 's'.

Contents: Jill.

Notes: Published in October 1946 at 9s. 6d. It has not been possible to trace the publisher's records and the printer has no records surviving from this period; the author has no recollection of ever having been told how many copies were printed. The British Library copy is receipt date stamped 31 December 1946.

The book was begun in autumn 1943 and finished about a year later. It was first sent to another publisher and rejected and was then sent to the Fortune Press, which accepted it. The original typescript was later thrown away by the author. The book was written under the influence of *The Senior Commoner*, by Julian Hall (cf. interview in *Tracks*, 1 (Summer 1967), p. 1).

(b) First Faber edition 1964

[fancy] JILL | A Novel | *by* | PHILIP LARKIN | FABER AND FABER | 24 Russell Square | London

Collation: $7\frac{3}{8} \times 4\frac{3}{4}$ in. [188 × 120 mm.] [A]–P⁸Q⁴, pp. [1–10] 11–19 [20] 21–247 [248].

[1–4]: blank. [5]: 'JILL'. [6]: 'by the same author | [star] | NOVEL | [two lines] | [star] | POETRY | [six lines]'. [7]: title page. [8]: '*First published in mcmxlvi | by The Fortune Press | First published in this edition mcmlxiv | by Faber and Faber Limited | 24 Russell Square London W. C. 1 | Printed in Great Britain | by Latimer Trend & Co Ltd Plymouth | All rights reserved*'.

[9]: 'To | JAMES BALLARD SUTTON'. [10]: blank. 11–19: introduction. [20]: author's note. 21–247: text. [248]: blank.

Binding: Bound in medium reddish-orange (37) cloth lettered across the spine in gold: 'JILL | by | Philip | Larkin | Faber'. White dust jacket printed in pink and black.

Paper: White wove unwatermarked paper.

Contents: Introduction. (pp. 11–19)
Jill.

Notes: Published 26 March 1964 in an edition of 3,000 copies at 21s., of which 2,000 copies were issued in the United States by the St. Martin's Press. Out of print in March 1971.
"... I have made a number of minor deletions but have added nothing and rewritten nothing, with the exception of a word here and there, and the reinstatement of a few mild obscenities to which the original printer objected."
(Introduction, p. 19). The printer's copy for this edition was a copy of the first edition with manuscript additions and corrections by the author; this was presented to the Bodleian Library in April 1964.

Reviews: E. Crispin. *Spectator*, CCXII (17 April 1964), 525.
J. Coleman. *Observer*, 29 March 1964, p. 22.
J. Connell. *Books of the Month*, May 1964, p. 4.
A. Curtis. *Sunday Telegraph*, 12 April 1964, p. 18.
S. Hill. *Coventry Evening Telegraph*, 2 April 1964, p. 11.
F. Hope. *Encounter*, XXII (May 1964), 74.
E. Jennings. *Listener*, LXXI (9 April 1964), 601.
S. Hugh-Jones. *New Statesman*, LXVII (3 April 1964), 533.
Times Literary Supplement, 16 April 1964, p. 305.

(c) First American issue   1964

[fancy] JILL | A Novel | *by* | PHILIP LARKIN | ST MARTIN'S PRESS | NEW YORK

Collation: The collation of the American issue is identical with that of the first Faber edition except on p. [8] which reads: '*Printed in Great Britain | Library of Congress | Catalog Card Number 64–17922 | © Philip Larkin 1964 | Originally published 1944 [sic] | Copyright in force in all countries | signatory to Berne Union | All rights reserved*'.

Binding: Bound in medium reddish-orange (37) cloth lettered across spine in gold: 'JILL | by | Philip | Larkin | ST MARTIN'S | PRESS'. White dust jacket printed in orange and black.

Paper: White wove unwatermarked paper.

Contents: As the first Faber edition.

Notes: Published 11 August 1964 in an issue of 2,286 copies at $4.50 and out of print in April 1968.

Reviews: B. Bergonzi. *New York Review of Books*, III (19 November 1964), 12.
       J. Bowen. *New York Times*, 27 September 1964, section 7, p. 54.
       W. B. Hill. *America*, CXI (28 November 1964), 722.
       E. Moon. *Saturday Review*, XXXXVII (19 September 1964), 49.

(d) First paperback edition   1975

[fancy] JILL | A Novel | *by* | PHILIP LARKIN | FABER AND FABER LTD | 3 Queen Square | London

Collation: 7¾×5 in. [196×127 mm.] [1–8]^{16}, pp. [1–10] 11–19 [20] 21–247 [248–56].
[1–4]: blank. [5]: 'JILL'. [6]: 'by the same author | [star] | [five lines] | [star] | [one line]'. [7]: title page. [8]: '*First published in 1946* | *by The Fortune Press* | *First published in this edition 1975* | *by Faber and Faber Limited* | *3 Queen Square London W. C. 1* | *Printed in Great Britain* | *Whitstable Litho Straker Brothers Ltd* | *All rights reserved* | *ISBN 0 571 10691 9* | [six lines] | © *Copyright Philip Larkin 1946*'. [9]: 'To | JAMES BALLARD SUTTON'. [10]: blank. 11–19: introduction. [20]: author's note. 21–247: text. [248–56]: blank.

Binding: Glued in a stiff white card cover printed down the spine: '[in grey] PHILIP LARKIN [in red] Jill [in white on a red panel] FABER'; and across the front cover: '[in grey with a red single-rule border] PHILIP LARKIN | [in white on a red panel] Jill'. The rear cover carries a description of the book in nine lines and the series title Faber Paperbacks.

Paper: White wove unwatermarked paper.

Contents: As the first Faber edition.

Notes: Published 3 March 1975 in an impression of 6,000 copies at £1.25p.

Reviews: A. Bold. *Tribune,* XXXIX (21 March 1975), 6–7.

    C. Bott. *Varsity,* 8 March 1975, p. 8.

    C. James. *New Statesman,* LXXXIX (21 March 1975), 383–4.

    J. Mortimer. *Isis,* 6 March 1975, pp. 22 and 24.

(e) First American edition   1976

JILL | a novel by | Philip Larkin | [device: elephant with wings within a double-rule circle] | The Overlook Press | Woodstock, New York

Collation: 8½ × 5¼ in. [215 × 135 mm.] [1–8]¹⁶, pp. [1–8] 9–19 [20] 21–247 [248–56].

[1–2]: blank. [3]: 'JILL'. [4]: 'by the same author | [star] | [five lines] | [star] | [one line]'. [5]: title page. [6]: 'First published in 1976 by | The Overlook Press | Lewis Hollow Road | Woodstock, New York 12498 | Copyright © 1946 by Philip Larkin | Copyright © 1976 by Philip Larkin | Library of Congress Catalog Card Number: 75-27292 | ISBN: 0–87951–038–2 | [nine lines] | Printed by The Studley Press, Inc.'. [7]: 'To | JAMES BALLARD SUTTON'. [8]: blank. 9–19: introduction. [20]: author's note. 21–247: text. [248–256]: blank.

Binding: Bound in black cloth lettered down the spine in gold: 'JILL PHILIP LARKIN [across the spine] The | Overlook | Press | [device]'. The device is blind stamped again on the lower-right front cover. Deep-yellow endpapers. White dust jacket printed in light yellow and reddish brown. Yellow and black head- and tail-bands.

Paper: Cream wove unwatermarked paper.

Contents: As the first Faber edition, with the addition of two new pages to the introduction on pp. 18–19.

Notes: Published 10 May 1976 in an edition of 2,500 copies at $8.95.

Reviews: M. Drabble. *New York Times,* 16 May 1976, section 7, p. 5.

    F. Kermode. *New York Review of Books,* XXIII (15 July 1976), 42–4.

A3   A GIRL IN WINTER   1947

(a) First edition

A GIRL IN WINTER | a novel by | PHILIP LARKIN | [ornament] | FABER AND FABER LTD | 24 Russell Square | London

Collation: $7\frac{1}{4}\times4\frac{3}{4}$ in. [185×123 mm.] [A]¹²B–H¹⁶, pp. [1–10] 11–63 [64–66] 67–174 [175–76] 177–248.
[1–2]: blank. [3]: 'A GIRL IN WINTER'. [4]: blank. [5]: title page. [6]: '*First published in Mcmxlvii* | *by Faber and Faber Limited* | *24 Russell Square London W. C. 1* | *Printed in Great Britain by* | *Purnell and Sons Limited* | *Paulton (Somerset) and London* | *All rights reserved*'. [7]: 'To | BRUCE MONTGOMERY'. [8]: blank. [9]: 'PART ONE'. [10]: blank. 11–63: text. [64]: blank. [65]: 'PART TWO'. [66]: blank. 67–174: text. [175]: 'PART THREE'. [176]: blank. 177–248: text.
The second and third printings collate [A]¹²B–P⁸.

Binding: Bound in strong greenish-blue (169) cloth lettered across the spine in gold: '*A* | *GIRL* | *IN* | *WINTER* | [snowflake ornament] | *Philip* | *Larkin* | *Faber*'. White dust jacket printed in red and grey. The second impression is bound in light blue (181) cloth with a dust jacket, redesigned by Margaret Wolpe, printed in red, black and green; the third impression has another redesigned dust jacket printed in blue, purple and black.

Paper: Cream wove unwatermarked paper. The second and third impressions are both printed on white wove unwatermarked paper.

Contents: A Girl in Winter.

Notes: Published 21 February 1947 in an impression of 5,000 copies at 8s. 6d. and out of print in November 1947. Reprinted and republished on 14 September 1956 in an impression of 2,060 copies and again reprinted in 1964 (2,500 copies).

Reviews: K. Amis. *Mandrake*, 1 (October 1947), 85–6.
D. George. *Tribune*, 538 (2 May 1947), 19.
S. P. B. Mais. *Oxford Mail*, 3 April 1947, p. 2.
A. Powell. *Daily Telegraph*, 28 February 1947, p. 3.
M. Sadleir. *Sunday Times*, 2 March 1947, p. 3.
E. Shanks. *Daily Dispatch* [Manchester], 27 March 1947, p. 2.
Times Literary Supplement, 22 March 1947, p. 125.

(b) First American issue   1962

A GIRL IN WINTER | *a novel by* | PHILIP LARKIN | [ornament] | ST MARTIN'S PRESS | NEW YORK

Collation: $7\frac{1}{4}\times4\frac{3}{4}$ in. [183×121 mm.] [A]¹²B–P⁸, pp. [1–10] 11–63 [64–66] 67–174 [175–76] 177–248.
As the first edition except for p. [6]: '*First published United States o*]

America 1962 | *Copyright © Philip Larkin 1957* | *First published in Great Britain* | *by Faber and Faber Limited 1957* | *Library of Congress Catalog Card Number: 62-17790* | *All rights reserved* | *Printed in Great Britain'*.

Binding: Bound in deep-blue (179) cloth lettered down the spine in silver: 'LARKIN *a girl in winter* ST MARTIN'S'. White shiny dust jacket printed in medium blue and silver.

Paper: White wove unwatermarked paper.

Contents: A Girl in Winter.

Notes: Published 8 January 1963 in an issue of 650 copies at $4.50 and out of print in August 1970. Another 1,000 copies of the bound, third British impression were also sold by St Martin's Press when the first 650 copies were exhausted.

Reviews: G. Gottlieb. *New York Herald Tribune*, 12 May 1963, p. 10.
A. Maples. *Washington Post*, 13 January 1963, p. G7.
E. MacNamara. *America*, CVIII (2 February 1963), 175.
P. Marsh. *Christian Science Monitor*, 27 June 1963, p. 11.
P. Pickrel. *Harpers*, CCXXVI (9 April 1963), 90 and 92.
Time, LXXXI (11 January 1963), 62.

(c) First paperback edition   1965

[The transcription of the title page is identical with that of the first edition.]

Collation: $7\frac{1}{4} \times 4\frac{3}{4}$ in. [184 × 120 mm.] 124 single sheets signed [A]^{12} B–P^8, p. [1–10] 11–63 [64–66] 67–174 [175–76] 177–248.
As the first edition except for p. [6]: '*First published in mcmlvii* | *by Faber and Faber Limited* | *24 Russell Square London W. C. 1* | *First published in this edition mcmlxv* | *Printed in Great Britain by* | *Latimer Trend & Co Ltd Whitstable* | *All rights reserved* | *Copyright © Philip Larkin 1957* | | [three lines]'.

Binding: Glued in a white card cover lettered on the spine: '[red band] [across in black] Philip | Larkin | [red square] | [down in black] *A GIRL IN WINTER* [in white on a grey panel] FABER'; on the front cover: '[red band] | [in black] *a novel by* | [red band] | [in black] *Philip Larkin* | [red band] | [in white on grey] *A Girl* | *in* | *Winter*'; down the front edge of the cover in white on a black panel: 'FABER paper covered EDITIONS'; this is repeated on the rear cover which carries, inside and out, lists of other titles in the series.

Paper: White wove unwatermarked paper.

Contents: A Girl in Winter

Notes: Published 25 February 1965 in an edition of 10,000 copies at 7s. 6d. and out of print in March 1972.

(d) Second paperback edition   1975

A GIRL IN WINTER|*a novel by*|PHILIP LARKIN|[ornament]|FABER AND FABER|3 Queen Square|London

Collation: 7¾×5 in. [196×126 mm.] [1–8]¹⁶, pp. [i–ii, 1–10] 11–63 [64–66] 67–174 [175–76] 177–248 [249–54].
[i–ii, 1–2]: blank. [3]: 'A GIRL IN WINTER'. [4]: 'by the same author| [star]|[five lines]|[star]|[one line]'. [5]: title page. [6]: '*First published in 1947*| *This edition published 1975*| *by Faber and Faber Limited*| *3 Queen Square, London, W.C. 1*| *Printed in Great Britain by*| *Whitstable Litho Straker Brothers Ltd.*| *All rights reserved*| *ISBN 0 571 10692 7*|[six lines]| © *Copyright Philip Larkin 1947*'. The remainder of the collation is identical with the first edition plus the final three blank leaves.

Binding: Glued in a white card cover lettered down the spine: '[in red] PHILIP LARKIN [in grey] A Girl in Winter [in white on a red panel] FABER'; and on the front cover: '[within a border of a single grey rule] [in red] PHILIP LARKIN [in white on a grey panel] A Girl|in Winter'. The rear cover carries on the outside a note on the book and on the inside reviews of other books by the same author.

Paper: White wove unwatermarked paper.

Contents: A Girl in Winter.

Notes: Published 3 March 1975 in an edition of 6,000 copies at £1.25.

Reviews: A Bold. *Tribune,* XXXIX (21 March 1975), 6–7.
      C. Bott. *Varsity,* 8 March 1975, p. 8.
      C. James. *New Statesman,* LXXXIX (21 March 1975), 383–4.
      J. Mortimer. *Isis,* 6 March 1975, pp. 22 and 24.

(e) First American edition   1976

A Girl in Winter|a novel by|PHILIP LARKIN|[device: elephant with wings within a double-rule circle]|The Overlook Press|Woodstock, New York
Collation: 8¹¹⁄₁₆×5⅜ in. [220×135 mm.] [1–8]¹⁶, pp. [1–10] 11–63 [64–66] 67–174 [175–176] 177–248 [249–256].

[1–2]: blank. [3]: '*A Girl in Winter*'. [4]: blank. [5]: title page. [6]: 'First published in 1976 by | The Overlook Press | Lewis Hollow Road | Woodstock, New York 12498 | Copyright © 1947 by Philip Larkin | Copyright © 1976 by Philip Larkin | Library of Congress Catalog Card Number: 75–27291 | ISBN: 0-87951-039-0 | [nine lines] | Printed by The Studley Press, Inc. | Dalton, Massachusetts 01226'. [7]: 'To | BRUCE MONTGOMERY'. [8]: blank. [9]: 'PART ONE'. [10]: blank. 11–63: text. [64]: blank. [65]: 'PART TWO'. [66]: blank. 67–174: text. [175]: 'PART THREE'. [176]: blank. 177–248: text. [249–256]: blank.

Binding: Bound in black cloth lettered down the spine in gold: '*A Girl in Winter Philip Larkin* [across the spine] [device] THE | OVERLOOK | PRESS'. The device is blind stamped again on the lower-right front cover. Deep-yellow endpapers. White dust jacket printed in black and pale reddish purple. Yellow and black head- and tail-bands.

Paper: White wove unwatermarked paper.

Contents: As the first Faber edition; a photolithographic reprint.

Notes: Published 25 October 1976 in an edition of 1,500 copies at $8.95.

Review: M. Amis. *New York Times*, 26 December 1976, section 7, pp. 2 and 16–17.

A4   XX POEMS   1951

[wrapper title] XX POEMS | PHILIP LARKIN | 1951

Collation: $8\frac{3}{4} \times 6\frac{3}{4}$ in. [209 × 159 mm.] One unsigned gathering of ten leaves, pp. [1–20].
[cover, recto]: title page. [cover, verso]: blank. [1]: '*This selection, written during the last | five years, is inscribed to Kingsley Amis.*' [2]: blank. [3–20]: text. [cover, recto and verso]: blank.

Binding: Stapled twice in a pale-pink (7) card cover lettered across the front cover as above.

Paper: White wove unwatermarked paper.

Contents:

  1 Wedding-wind: The wind blew all my wedding-day . . .
      Reprinted in TLD and *Recognitions*, Winter 1971.

II   Modesties: Words as plain as hen-birds' wings . . . Reprinted in *Humberside*, Autumn 1958, *Poetry Book Society Bulletin*, February 1964 and *Encounter*, March 1964.

III Always too eager for the future, we . . . Reprinted in *Departure*, Spring 1955 and TLD ("Next, please").

IV   Even so distant, I can taste the grief . . . Reprinted in TLD ("Deceptions").

V   Latest face, so effortless . . . Reprinted in the *Spectator*, 5 March 1954 and TLD.

VI   Arrival: Morning, a glass door, flashes . . .

VII Since the majority of me . . .

VIII Spring: Green-shadowed people sit, or walk in rings . . . Reprinted in *Listen*, Summer 1954 and TLD.

IX   Waiting for breakfast, while she brushed her hair . . . Reprinted in *Poetry Book Society Bulletin*, July 1956 and NS (Faber edition).

X   Two portraits of sex. 1 Oils: Sun. Tree. Beginning. God in a thicket. Crown . . .

XI   2 Etching: Endlessly, time-honoured irritant . . . Reprinted in *Listen*, Summer 1954, and TLD ("Dry-point").

XII On longer evenings . . . Reprinted in TLD ("Coming").

XIII Since we agreed to let the road between us . . . Reprinted in *Departure*, Summer 1955, and TLD ("No road").

XIV If my darling were once to decide . . .Reprinted in *Fantasy poets*, No. 21, TLD, and *Shenandoah*, Spring 1955.

XV   Who called love conquering . . .

XVI The widest prairies have electric fences . . . Reprinted in *Spectator*, 2 October 1953, and TLD ("Wires").

XVII The dedicated: Some must employ the scythe . . .

XVIII Wants: Beyond all this, the wish to be alone . . . Reprinted in TLD, *Sunday Times*, 21 January 1962, and *Recognitions*, Winter 1971.

XIX There is an evening coming in . . . Reprinted in TLD ("Going"), and *Recognitions*, Winter 1971.

XX   At grass: The eye can hardly pick them out . . . Reprinted in *Fantasy Poets*, No. 21, TLD, and *Recognitions*, Winter 1971.

Notes: Privately printed for the author in an edition of 100 copies "by Carswells of Belfast, and . . . a Mr Hennessey saw me about it, saying they would print it in '10p Old Face Roman' . . . The hundred copies arrived on the 27th April [1951] . . . " (Larkin in a letter to Bloomfield).

Most of the copies were sent by the author to prominent litt. figures who generally did not acknowledge receipt, insufficient stamps having been put on the envelopes because postage rates had just been raised.

Review: D. J. Enright. *Month,* n.s.VI (November 1951), 309.

A5   THE FANTASY POETS No. 21   1954

[all within a very deep-red double- (outer thick, inner thin) | border]
THE FANTASY POETS | PHILIP | LARKIN | NUMBER TWENTY ONE

Collation: 8¼×5¼ in. [210×133 cm.] One unsigned gathering of four leaves, pp. [1–8].

[1]: title page. [2–7]: text. [8]: '[four-line note on the author] | Editors: GEORGE MACBETH | 1954 OSCAR MELLOR | [rule] | 'The Fantasy Poets' series is issued by the Oxford University Poetry | Society (enquiries should be addressed to the Secretary). Printed and | published by the Fantasy Press at Swinford, Eynsham, Oxford. | PRICE NINEPENCE'.

Binding: Stapled twice.

Paper: White wove paper watermarked: '*Plus* | *Fabric*'.

Contents: Lines on a young lady's photograph album: At last you yielded up the album, which . . . Reprinted in Q, Autumn 1955, and TLD.

     Whatever happened?: At once whatever happened starts receding . . . Reprinted in TLD.

     If, my darling: If my darling were once to decide . . . Reprinted from *XX Poems.*

     Arrivals, departures: This town has docks where channel boats come sidling . . . Reprinted in Q, Autumn 1955, and TLD.

     At grass: The eye can hardly pick them out . . . Reprinted from *XX Poems.*

Notes: Published in March 1954 in an edition of about 300 copies. (For further notes on the series see J. Cotton 'The Fantasy Press' *Private Library,* 2nd series, II, 1 (Spring 1969), pp. 3–13.) Set in 10 pt Times New Roman; out of print by the end of 1954.

Review: A. Hartley. *Spectator,* CXCVII (2 April 1954), 411.

A6   THE LESS DECEIVED

(a) First edition

THE LESS DECEIVED | Poems | by | PHILIP LARKIN | THE MARVELL PRESS

Collation: 8½ × 5½ in. [215 × 140 mm.] [1–6]⁴, pp. [1–10] 11–43 [44–8].
[1]: 'THE LESS DECEIVED'. [2]: 'by Philip Larkin | A GIRL IN WINTER | (Faber & Faber)'. [3]: title page. [4]: '*First published in October 1955* | *by* | *The Marvell Press* | *at 253 Hull Road* | *Hessle* | *East Yorkshire* | *All rights reserved*'. [5]: acknowledgements. [6]: blank. [7]: contents. [8]: blank. [9]: 'To | Monica Jones'. [10]: blank. 11–43: text. [44–45]: list of subscribers before publication . . . [final two lines on p. 45] 'Set in 11 pt. Garamond type on 12 pt. and printed by Villiers Publica- | tions, Holloway, London, on Abbey Mills antique laid paper.' [40–48]: blank.

The 4th impression pages [1–12] 13–45 (46–48) with all the contents thus moved back two page numbers; the words '© *The Marvell Press*' first occur on the verso of the title page. These changes also apply in the 5th and 6th impressions.

Binding: Bound in medium yellow-green (120) cloth lettered down the spine in gold: 'THE LESS DECEIVED PHILIP LARKIN'; the spine has a strip of stiffening mull inserted. Dust jacket of light grey red (18) printed in green and black, with price given as 6s., and the rear wrapper printed in black only. A later binding has no strip of stiffening mull bound in the spine; some copies of this issue have the price on the dust jacket raised by means of a white stick-on label to 7s. 6d. The soft cover edition is glued in a plain yellow grey card wrapper with the dust jacket glued on as a cover, omits the list of subscribers and the price is given as 6s.

The 5th impression is bound in rough medium-olive-green (125) cloth lettered down the spine in gold: 'THE LESS DECEIVED PHILIP LARKIN THE MARVELL PRESS'; medium-pink (5) dust jacket printed in black.

The 6th impression is bound in deep-pink (3) cloth and lettered as the 5th impression; pale purplish-pink (252) dust jacket printed in light reddish purple and black.

Paper: White laid paper watermarked in Gothic: '[crown] | Abbey Mills | Greenfield'.

Contents: Lines on a young lady's photograph album: At last you yielded up the album, which . . . First printed in *Fantasy poets*, No. 21.

Wedding-wind: The wind blew all my wedding-day . . . First printed in *XX Poems*.

Places, loved ones: No, I have never found . . . First printed in *Spectator*, 7 January 1955 ("Times, places, loved ones").

Coming: On longer evenings . . . First printed in *XX Poems*.

Reasons for attendance: The trumpet's voice, loud and authoritative . . .

Dry-point: Endlessly, time-honoured irritant . . . First printed in *XX Poems*.

Next, please: Always too eager for the future, we . . . First printed in *XX Poems*.

Going: There is an evening coming in . . . First printed in *XX Poems*.

Wants: Beyond all this, the wish to be alone . . . First printed in *XX Poems*.

Maiden name: Marrying left your maiden name disused . . .

Born yesterday: Tightly-folded bud . . . First printed in *Spectator*, 30 July 1954. Dedicated to Sally Amis.

Whatever happened: At once whatever happened starts receding . . . First printed in *Fantasy Poets*, No. 21.

No road: Since we agreed to let the road between us . . . First printed in *XX Poems*.

Wires: The widest prairies have electric fences . . . First printed in *XX Poems*.

Church going: Once I am sure there's nothing going on . . . Reprinted in the *Spectator*, 18 November 1955.

Age: My age fallen away like white swaddling . . . First printed in the *Spectator*, 2 July 1954.

Myxomatosis: Caught in the centre of a soundless field . . . First printed in the *Spectator*, 26 November 1954.

Toads: Why should I let the toad *work* . . . First printed in *Listen*, Summer 1954.

Poetry of departures: Sometimes you hear, fifth-hand . . . First printed in *Poetry and Audience*, June 1954 and reprinted in *Listen*, Winter 1954.

Triple time: This empty street, this sky to blandness scoured

... First printed in *Poetry and Audience*, 28 January 1954 and reprinted in the *Spectator*, 30 April 1954.

Spring: Green-shadowed people sit, or walk in rings ... First printed in *XX Poems*.

Deceptions: Even so distant, I can taste the grief ... First printed in *XX Poems*.

I remember, I remember: Coming up England by a different line ... First printed in *Platform*, Autumn 1955.

Absences: Rain patters on a sea that tilts and sighs ... Some, presumably the earliest, copies of the first issue of the first impression read 'floor' for 'sea' in the first line of this poem.

Latest face: Latest face, so effortless ... First printed in *XX Poems*.

If, my darling: If my darling were once to decide ... First printed in *XX Poems*.

Skin: Obedient daily dress ... First printed in the *Spectator*, 2 July 1954.

Arrivals, departures: This town has docks where channel boats come sidling ... First printed in *Fantasy Poets*, No. 21.

At grass: The eye can hardly pick them out ... First printed in *XX Poems*.

Notes: In 1954 George Hartley, the editor of the magazine *Listen*, wrote to Philip Larkin to ask him if he had enough poems for a book. Early in 1955 Larkin sent him the typescript of a collection entitled *Various Poems* which Hartley accepted and the book took almost the rest of 1955 to print and bind. Since Hartley disliked the projected title Larkin retitled one poem, "Deceptions", and gave the poem's original title to the entire collection. The Marvell Press distributed forms inviting subscriptions to the volume in June 1955; the closing date for subscriptions was 15 September and publication was planned for October. The volume was actually sent out to subscribers late in November 1955 at the price of 6s. It was mentioned in *The Times* in a review of the year's literature on 22 December and this prompted the rapid sale of the rest of the subscription issue, 300 copies with flat spine and the misprint 'floor' for 'sea' on p. 38. A further 400 copies were bound up, with rounded spines, but the stocks of the book were sold out by April 1956. When a reprint was ordered it was found that the original type had been broken up in mistake and it was necessary to reset the entire book. The reset edition appeared in soft wrappers in August 1956 still at the price of 6s. The clearest account of the somewhat complicated history of the book is to be found on the sleeve of the first issue of the recording of the poet reading the poems, *The Less Deceived*, Listen LPV [1], and is by the poet himself, although unsigned.

A careful comparison of the first edition with the reset edition in soft covers reveals very few differences, but it may be useful to list these now: p. 30, line 23, the terminal exclamation mark is in italic in the first edition but in roman in the soft cover edition; p. 40, line 14, the comma at the end of the line is omitted in the soft cover edition; and, most easily recognizable, the page numbers in the soft cover edition are in a different face (Garamond) from the first edition where they are actually set in Linotype Baskerville.

The so-called "Second edition" of the book is dated January 1956, and is a part of the first impression. (This "Second edition" is dated February 1956 on the verso of the title pages of the so-called Third, Fourth and Fifth editions.) The "Third edition" is dated July 1956 and was sold at 10s. 6d.; the "Fourth edition" is dated January 1958 with a similar price; the "Fifth edition" is dated January 1962 and was priced at 12s. 6d.; and the "Sixth edition" is dated May 1966 and was priced at 15s. initially, although this was later raised. Pages [4] and [6] of this impression were reset, and the text is that of the first impression, while the text of the "Fourth" and "Fifth" editions follows that of the soft cover edition. Information from the printer and a study of his records makes the position somewhat clearer.

First impression

The first impression of the book was quoted for on 14 March 1955, invoiced on 24 November 1955, and consisted of 700 copies of which 300 were bound. From these 300 bound copies were dispatched the 120 or so subscribers' volumes and the remainder were sold in the usual fashion. (The early copies of this impression are bound with flat spines.) On 29 February 1956 the printer invoiced the publisher for the cost of binding 400 more copies; these copies comprised the remainder of the 'First edition' and the copies of what is described on the verso of the title page as the "Second edition", but which were actually printed at the same time as the first and form part of the first impression. Copies from the first impression have the misprint "floor" for "sea" in the first line of the poem "Absences" on p. 38 and have a list of subscribers before publication on pp. [44–45].

Second impression

The second impression of the book was invoiced on 31 August 1956 and consisted of 1,320 copies in soft covers. This is actually a second edition and a new setting of type and is characterized by the three changes listed above and the correction of the misprint on p. 38. The verso of the title page makes no mention of its being the second impression, but the inner flap of the rear wrapper carries extracts from reviews of the book's first impression. In the bibliographical history of the book carried on the verso of the title page in subsequent printings this second printing is described as the "Third Edition" and is dated July 1956.

Third impression

The third impression consisted of 1,540 copies and was invoiced on 22 March 1958; it is described as the "Fourth Edition" and is dated January 1958. The printer's bill also includes a sum for the printing of a special dust jacket for copies exported to the United States for sale, presumably, through the St. Martin's Press. The text of this printing follows that of the second, with altered pagination as described above.

Fourth impression

The fourth impression consisted of 2,000 copies of which 500 were immediately bound and sent to Hull, the remainder being bound at a later date. This is described as the "Fifth Edition" and the text follows that of the second impression with the altered pagination.

Fifth impression

The fifth impression consisted of 4,000 copies and is described as the "Sixth Edition". The text follows that of the first printing, but with the altered pagination.

The title went out of print in this edition late in 1973.

The book had been rejected by The Dolmen Press before it was accepted by The Marvell Press. Mr George Hartley still possesses the original copy and proofs.

Reviews: A. Alvarez. *Partisan Review*, XXV (Fall 1958), 603–9.
F. W. Bateson. *Essays in Criticism*, VII (January 1957), 76–80.
H. Chambers. *Phoenix*, 3 (Spring 1960), 22–3.
D. Davie. *Irish Writing*, 34 (Spring 1956), 62–4.
R. Fuller. *London Magazine*, III (April 1956), 84–8.
G. S. Fraser. *New Statesman*, LI (21 January 1956), 79–80.
A. Hartley. *Spectator*, CLXXXXVI (8 June 1956), 801–2.
D. K[eene]. *Departure*, III (Spring 1956), 22–3.

C. Levenson. *Delta*, 8 (Spring 1956), 26–8.

N. Lewis. *Observer*, 5 February 1956, p. 11.

Listener, LVI (15 November 1956), 809. (See also subsequent letter by G. Hough on p. 844 and reply on p. 885.)

S. F. Morse. *Poetry*, LXXXIX (December 1956), 196–7.

A. Ridler. *Manchester Guardian*, 17 February 1956, p. 6.

H. S[hoosmith]. *Humberside*, XII (Autumn 1956), 33–8.

J. Silkin. *Stand*, 12 (Winter 1956/7), [34].

G. Taylor. *Time and Tide*, 28 January 1956, pp. 113–14.

Times Literary Supplement, 16 December 1955, p. 762.

D. Wright. *Encounter*, VII (October 1956), 74–8.

K. Young. *Daily Telegraph*, 6 April 1956, p. 8.

(b) First American edition 1960

THE LESS DECEIVED | Poems | by | PHILIP LARKIN | ST MARTIN'S PRESS · NEW YORK

Collation: 8½ × 5¼ in. [215 × 134 mm.] [1–3]⁸, pp. [1–12] 13–45 [46–48]. [1–2]: blank. [3]: half title. [4]: blank. [5]: title page. [6]: '*Copyright* © *The Marvell Press 1955, 1960* | *All rights reserved* | [four lines italic] | *Manufactured in the United States of America*'. [7]: acknowledgements. [8]: blank. [9]: contents. [10]: blank. [11]: 'To | Monica Jones'. [12]: blank. 13–45: text. [46–48]: blank.

The second printing measures 8½ × 5½ in. [216 × 140 mm.].

Binding: Bound in strong red (12) cloth lettered down the spine: '[two gold ornaments] [in silver] THE LESS DECEIVED [four gold ornaments] [in silver] PHILIP LARKIN [gold ornament] [in gold] ST MARTIN'S'; and across the front cover: '[four silver ornaments] | [in gold] PHILIP LARKIN | [four silver ornaments]'. Dark red endpapers. Light-grey dust jacket printed in dark red.

Paper: Cream laid paper watermarked, in cursive, '*Utopian*'. The second printing is on cream laid paper, unwatermarked.

Contents: As the English edition. The first word of the poem "Toads" on p. 32 is misprinted as "What...", and there are the following additional misprints:— p. 13, line 3, for "thick pages" read "thick black pages"; p. 15, line 19, for "you" read "joy"; p. 18, line 13, for "bell" read "sound"; p. 19, line 8, for "bright-blown" read "bright blown"; p. 20, line 1, for "for future" read "for the future"; p. 29, line 15, for "whom" read "which"; p. 45, line 21 for "stone" read "stole".

Notes: Published 22 May 1960 in an impression of 1,131 copies at $3.50 and reprinted in November 1965 (1,500 copies) when the price was raised to $3.95. Out of print in January 1972. Some copies of the third printing of the English edition, with specially printed dust jackets, had been sold in the United States by St. Martin's Press prior to the publication of this American edition.

Reviews: L. Bogan. *New Yorker*, xxxiv (13 September 1958), 158–63 [New York edition 146, 149–51].
J. Ciardi. *Saturday Review*, xli (27 September 1958). 31–2.
A. Derleth. *Voices*, 168 (January–April 1959), 48–51.
N. K. Dorn. *San Francisco Chronicle*, 23 November 1958, section CB, p. 13.
D. Hall. *Shenandoah*, vii (Summer 1956), 45–52.
M. L. Rosenthal. *Nation*, clxxxviii (16 May 1959), 457–8.
H. Shapiro. *New York Times*, 28 September 1958, section 7, p. 40.
J. Tobin. *Spirit*, xxvi (September 1959), 124.

(c) First paperback edition   1974

THE LESS DECEIVED | Poems | by | PHILIP LARKIN | THE MARVELL PRESS

Collation: 7¾ × 5 in. [196 × 128 mm.] [1–3]⁸, pp. [1–12] 13–45 [46–48]. [1–2]: blank. [3]: half title. [4]: blank. [5]: title page. [6]: '*First published in October 1955* | *by* | *The Marvell Press* | *First published in this edition 1973* | *All rights reserved* | *Printed and bound in Great Britain by* | REDWOOD BURN LIMITED | *Trowbridge & Esher*'. [7]: acknowledgements. [8]: blank. [9]: contents. [10]: blank. [11]: 'To | Monica Jones'. [12]: blank. 13–45: text. [46–48]: blank.

Binding: Glued in a white card cover lettered down the spine in medium violet (211): 'THE LESS DECEIVED PHILIP LARKIN THE MARVELL PRESS'. The front wrapper has a photograph of Larkin's face in medium violet and across this in white: 'PHILIP LARKIN | THE | LESS | DECEIVED | THE MARVELL PRESS'. The outer rear wrapper carries advertisements for cassette recordings of Larkin reading *The Less Deceived* and *The Whitsun Weddings*; the front inner wrapper carries a comment on TLD by Robert Lowell, and the rear inner wrapper advertises other publications by the Press.

Paper: White wove unwatermarked paper.

Contents: A photolithographic reprint of the first American edition, with the misprint in the first line of the poem "Toads" on p. 32; and all the others.

Notes: Published in March 1974 in an impression of 5,000 copies at 80p.

A7   THE WHITSUN WEDDINGS   1964

(a) First edition

THE | WHITSUN WEDDINGS | poems by | PHILIP LARKIN | FABER AND FABER | 24 Russell Square | London

Collation: $8\frac{1}{2} \times 5\frac{1}{4}$ in. [215 × 135 mm.] [A]–C⁸, pp. [1–6] 7–46 [47–48]. [1–2]: blank. [3]: half title. [4]: 'by the same author | [twelve lines]'. [5]: title page. [6]: '*First published in mcmlxiv | by Faber and Faber Limited | 24 Russell Square London W C 1 | Printed in Great Britain | by the Bowering Press Plymouth | All rights reserved | © 1964 by Philip Larkin*'. 7–8: contents. 9–46: text. [47–48]: blank.

Binding: Bound in dark purplish-red (259) cloth lettered down the. spine in gold: '*The Whitsun Weddings* [dot] *Philip Larkin* [dot] *Faber*' Pale orange-yellow dust jacket printed in red, green and black.

The third impression is bound in shiny strong-red (12) cloth mottled with black, with a cream dust jacket; the fourth impression is bound in shiny deep-red (13) fine diaper cloth.

Paper: White wove unwatermarked paper.

Contents: Here: Swerving east, from rich industrial shadows . . . First printed in *New Statesman*, 24 November 1961.
Mr Bleaney: 'This was Mr Bleaney's room. He stayed . . . First printed in *Listener*, 8 September 1955, and reprinted in *New World Writing*, November 1956.
Nothing to be said: For nations vague as weed . . . First printed in *London Magazine*, February 1962.
Love songs in age: She kept her songs, they took so little space . . . First printed in *Poetry*, *1960*.

Naturally the Foundation will bear your expenses: Hurrying to catch my Comet . . . First printed in *Twentieth Century*, July 1961, and reprinted in *Partisan Review*, Summer 1964.

Broadcast: Giant whispering and coughing from . . . First printed in *Listener*, 25 January 1962.

Faith healing: Slowly the women file to where he stands . . . First printed in *Listener*, 21 July 1960, and reprinted in *Shenandoah*, Winter 1962.

For Sidney Bechet: That note you hold, narrowing and rising, shakes . . . First printed in *Ark*, November 1956 and reprinted in *Listen*, Autumn 1962.

Home is so sad: Home is so sad. It stays as it was left . . . First printed in *Listener*, 23 January 1964.

Toads revisited: Walking around in the park . . . First printed in *Spectator*, 23 November 1962, and reprinted in *New York Review of Books*, 14 January 1965.

Water: If I were called in . . . First printed in *Listen*, Summer–Autumn 1957, and reprinted in *Poetry and Drama Magazine*, 1958 and *Recognitions*, Winter 1971.

The Whitsun weddings: That Whitsun, I was late getting away . . . First printed in *Encounter*, June 1959.

Self's the man: Oh, no one can deny . . .

Take one home for the kiddies: On shallow straw, in shade-less glass . . . First printed in *Listener*, 5 December 1963.

Days: What are days for? . . . First printed in *Listen*, Summer–Autumn 1957, and reprinted in *Poetry and Drama Magazine*, 1958 and *Recognitions*, Winter 1971.

MCMXIV: Those long uneven lines . . . First printed in *Saturday Book*, 1960 and reprinted in *Poetry Quarterly*, October–December 1961.

Talking in bed: Talking in bed ought to be easiest . . . First printed in *Texas Quarterly*, Winter 1960.

The large cool store: The large cool store selling cheap clothes . . . First printed in *Times Literary Supplement*, 14 July 1961.

A study of reading habits: When getting my nose in a book . . . First printed in *Critical Quarterly*, Winter 1960.

As bad as a mile: Watching the shied core . . . First printed in *Audit*, 28 March 1961, and reprinted in *Listener*, 21 December 1963.

Ambulances: Closed like confessionals, they thread . . . First printed in *London Magazine*, April 1961, and reprinted in *Atlantic*, December 1961 and *Observer* [colour magazine], 14 August 1966.

The importance of elsewhere: Lonely in Ireland, since it was not home . . . First printed in *Listener*, 8 September 1955 and reprinted in *Humberside*, Autumn 1956 and *Listen*, Spring 1958.

Sunny Prestatyn: *Come to Sunny Prestatyn* . . . First printed in *London Magazine*, January 1963.

First sight: Lambs that learn to walk in snow . . . First printed in *Times Educational Supplement*, 13 July 1956 ("At first").

Dockery and Son: 'Dockery was junior to you . . . First printed in *Listener*, 11 April 1963.

Ignorance: Strange to know nothing, never to be sure . . . First printed in *Listen*, Summer 1956.

Reference back: *That was a pretty one*, I heard you call . . . First printed in *Listen*, Autumn 1955 ("Referred back"), and reprinted in *Paris Review*, Summer 1958.

Wild oats: About twenty years ago . . . First printed in *The Review*, February 1963.

Essential beauty: In frames as large as rooms that face all ways . . . First printed in *Spectator*, 5 October 1962, and reprinted in *The Balkite*, November 1962.

Send no money: Standing under the fobbed . . . First printed in *Observer*, 18 November 1962.

Afternoons: Summer is fading . . . First printed in *Listen*, Spring 1960 ("Before tea").

An Arundel tomb: Side by side, their faces blurred . . . First printed in *London Magazine*, May 1956 and reprinted in *Poetry and Audience*, 16 November 1956, and *Torch*, Easter 1957.

Notes: Published 28 February 1964 in an impression of 3,910 copies at 12s. 6d., and reprinted in April 1964 (3,000 copies), August 1965 (3,000 copies), July 1968 (3,000 copies) and January 1971 (2,500 copies). The book was the spring choice of the Poetry Book Society, and on its publication Larkin was awarded by the Arts Council a prize of £250 for "the best book of original English verse by a living poet published from July 1962 to June 1965" (*The Times*, 30 September 1965, p. 14).

Subsequent to its publication, on 5 May 1965, Larkin was awarded the Queen's Gold Medal for Poetry.

Reviews: A. Alvarez. *Observer*, 1 March 1964, p. 27.

J. Betjeman. *Listener*, LXXI (19 March 1964), 483. (See also Gavin Ewart's poem "The blurb" in his *No fool like an old fool* (London, Gollancz, 1976) p. 58.)

H. Chambers. *Phoenix*, 10 (Spring 1964), 38–43.

A. Curtis. *Sunday Telegraph*, 12 April 1964, p. 18.

P. Dale. *Agenda*, III (September 1964), 28–30.

D. J. Enright. *New Statesman*, LXVII (28 February 1964), 331–2.

C. Falck. *The Review*, 14 (December 1964), 3–11.

Z. Ghose. *Ambit*, 20 (1964), 53–4.

I. Hamilton. *London Magazine*, IV (May 1964), 70–4.

P. Hobsbawm. *Outposts*, 61 (Summer 1964), 21–3.

J. Holloway. *Spectator*, CCXVII (28 February 1964), 288.

F. Hope. *Encounter*, XXII (May 1964), 72–4.

E. Jennings. *Daily Telegraph*, 30 July 1964, p. 18.

B. Kennelly. *Dubliner*, III (Summer 1964), 88–9.

G. Melly. *Sunday Times*, 1 March 1964, p. 37.

J. M. Newton. *Cambridge Quarterly*, 1 (Winter 1965/6), 96–101.

D. Parker. *Poetry Review*, LV (Summer 1964), 110–11.

J. Raban. *Torchlight* [University of Hull], 89 (5 May 1964), p. 5.

M. Seymour-Smith. *Scotsman* [week-end magazine], 23 May 1964, p. 6.

Times Literary Supplement, 12 March 1964, p. 216.

(b) First American edition   1964

The | WHITSUN | WEDDINGS | poems by | Philip Larkin | [ornament] | [device: a house] | Random House | New York

Collation: 8¼ × 5½ in. [210 × 140 mm.] [1–3]⁸, pp. [1–6] 7–46 [47–48]. [1–2]: blank. [3]: half title .[4]: '*Books by* Philip Larkin | *Poetry* | The North Ship | The Less Deceived | The Whitsun Weddings | *Novels* | Jill | A Girl in Winter'. [5]: title page. [6]: '© *Copyright, 1960, 1961, 1962, 1964, by Philip Larkin.* | [seven lines] | MANUFACTURED IN THE UNITED STATES OF AMERICA'. 7–8: contents. 9–46: text. [47–48]: blank.

Binding: Bound in strong-red (12) rough cloth lettered down the spine in gold: '*THE WHITSUN WEDDINGS* [solid gold spot] *PHILIP LARKIN* RANDOM HOUSE'; device blind stamped on the lower-right front cover. Top edge stained green. The dust jacket is pale yellowish-pink printed in red, green and black with a photograph on the rear and biographical data by the author on the rear inner flap.

Paper: White wove unwatermarked paper.

Contents: As the English edition; a photolithographic reprint.

Notes: Published 23 September 1964 in an impression of 2,023 copies at $4, and reprinted in July 1966 (1,525 copies). Out of print in 1973.

Reviews: L. Bogan. *New Yorker,* XLI (10 April 1965), 193–4.
R. F. Deen. *Commonweal,* LXXXI (25 December 1964), 459.
H. Hobson. *Christian Science Monitor,* 23 April 1964, p. 11.
T. Kinsella. *New York Times,* 20 December 1964, section 7, p. 4.
L. Martz. *Yale Review,* LIV (June 1965), 605.
C. Ricks. *New York Review of Books.* III 14 January 1965), 10–11.
R. D. Spector. *Saturday Review,* XLVIII (13 February 1965), 47.
W. Stafford. *Poetry,* CVI (July 1965), 294–5.
Time, LXXXV (19 February 1965), 67–8.
Virginia Quarterly Review, XLI (Winter 1965), xvi.

(c) First American paperback issue   1964

[The transcription of the title page is identical with that of the first American edition.]

Collation: As the first American edition.

Binding: Glued in a white card cover printed in pale orange yellow (73) lettered down the spine: '[in red] *THE WHITSUN WEDDINGS* [green: dot] *PHILIP LARKIN* [in red] RANDOM HOUSE'; and across the front cover: '[green rule] | [red fancy shaded, with a vertical red rule to the right] *THE* | *WHITSUN* | *WEDDINGS* | [green rule] | [red fancy shaded, with a vertical red rule to the left] *PHILIP* | *LARKIN* | [green rule] | A RANDOM HOUSE BOOK $1.95'. The rear wrapper carries an appreciation by Robert Penn Warren.

Paper: White wove unwatermarked paper.

Contents: As the first American edition.

Notes: Published 23 September 1964 in an issue of 4,190 copies at $1.95.

(d) First English paperback issue 1971

THE|WHITSUN WEDDINGS|poems by|PHILIP LARKIN|FABER AND FABER|3 Queen Square|London

Collation: 7¾×5 in. [197×127 mm.] [A]–C⁸, pp. [1–6] 7–46 [47–48]. [1–2]: blank. [3]: half title. [4]: 'by the same author|[ten lines]'. [5]: title page. [6]: '*First published in 1964 by Faber and Faber Limited*|*First published in this edition 1971*|*Printed in Great Britain*|*by the Bowering Press Plymouth*|*All rights reserved*|ⓒ *1964 by Philip Larkin*|ISBN 0 571 09710 3 (Faber Paper Covered Editions)|ISBN 0 571 05750 0 (Hard Bound Edition)|CONDITIONS OF SALE|[five lines of italic]'. 7–8: contents. 9–46: text. [47–48]: blank. The second impression measures 192×127 mm.

Binding: Glued in a white card cover lettered down the spine in black: '[continuation of red and green rules from the front wrapper] PHILIP LARKIN|[continuation of red and green rules from the front wrapper] THE WHITSUN WEDDINGS [in white on a black panel] FABER'; and across the front wrapper: '[green rule]|[red rule]|[fancy shaded] *PHILIP*|*LARKIN*|[green rule]|[red rule]|[fancy shaded] *THE*|*WHITSUN*|*WEDDINGS*|[green rule]|[red rule]'and down the outside edge in white on a black panel: 'FABER paper covered EDITIONS'. This panel is repeated on the rear wrapper which also carries the titles of other books in the series. The inside front wrapper carries a note on the book and the inside rear wrapper notes other books by Larkin. The 1973 reprint changes the wording on the panels along the outside edges of the wrappers to read, in black on white: 'Faber paper covered editions'.

Paper: White wove unwatermarked paper.

Notes: Published 17 May 1971 in an impression of 8,500 copies at 35p, and reprinted in June 1973 (10,000 copies).

A8   ALL WHAT JAZZ   1970

(a) First edition

All What Jazz | [long rule] | A Record Diary 1961–68 | PHILIP LARKIN | FABER AND FABER London

Collation: 7¾×5 in. [197×127 mm.] [A] B [C] D–S⁸, pp. [i–xiv], 1–272 [273–74].
[i–ii]: blank. [iii]: half title. [iv]: blank. [v]: title page. [vi]: '*First published in 1970 | by Faber and Faber Limited | 24 Russell Square London W C 1 | Printed in Great Britain by | Hull Printers Ltd., Willerby, Hull, Yorkshire | All rights reserved | SBN 571 09240 3 | © Philip Larkin 1970*'. [vii]: 'To | DONALD MITCHELL'. [viii]: blank. [ix–xii]: contents. [xiii]: epigraphs. [xiv]: textual note. 1–18: introduction. 19–255: text. 256–72: records reviewed. [273–74]: blank.

Binding: Bound in strong brown (55) cloth lettered down the spine in gold: 'ALL WHAT JAZZ | [long rule] | Philip Larkin [across the foot of the spine] FABER'. Shiny white dust jacket printed in blue and black.

Paper: White wove unwatermarked paper.

Contents: Introduction.
>   The white world. First printed in *Daily Telegraph*, 11 February 1961 ("Echoes of the Gatsby era").
>   Having a ball. First printed in *Daily Telegraph*, 11 March 1961 ("Benny's immortal hour").
>   The persistence of the blues. First printed in *Daily Telegraph*, 15 April 1961 ("The growth of the blues").
>   Bands across the sea. First printed in *Daily Telegraph*, 13 May 1961.
>   Bechet and Bird. First printed in *Daily Telegraph*, 10 June 1961 ("Better than the best").
>   Cool Britannia. First printed in *Daily Telegraph*, 15 July 1961 ("Folk heroes in bowlers").
>   Panassié stomps. First printed in *Daily Telegraph*, 12 August 1961 ("Putting the moderns in their place").
>   Make me a palate. First printed in *Daily Telegraph*, 9 September 1961 ("Post-holiday recuperation").

Survival of the hottest. First printed in *Daily Telegraph*, 14 October 1961.

Looking back at Louis. First printed in *Daily Telegraph*, 11 November 1961 ("Trumpet preliminary").

Horn in a dilemma. First printed in *Daily Telegraph*, 9 December 1961 ("Horn of a dilemma").

Rose-red-light city. First printed in *Daily Telegraph*, 13 January 1962 ("The spell of Basin street").

Without the Duke. First printed in *Daily Telegraph*, 10 February 1962 ("Ellington minus the Duke").

After the moderns. First printed in *Daily Telegraph*, 10 March 1962 ("Young revolutionaries").

Ranging through the decades. First printed in *Daily Telegraph*, 16 April 1962 ("Old hands in new sleeves").

Armstrong to Parker. First printed in *Daily Telegraph*, 14 May 1962 ("Contrasting equals").

Up from the south. First printed in *Daily Telegraph*, 16 June 1962 ("Voices from the south").

'You're a genius!' First printed in *Daily Telegraph*, 14 July 1962 ("Grace notes from outer space").

Jazz as a way of life. First printed in *Daily Telegraph*, 11 August 1962 ("Fact and fiction").

Big noise from yesterday. First printed in *Daily Telegraph*, 8 September 1962.

Billie's golden years. First printed in *Daily Telegraph*, 17 October 1962 ("Holiday in spring and summer").

Jam yesterday. First printed in *Daily Telegraph*, 10 November 1962.

Don't go 'way nobody. First printed in *Daily Telegraph*, 15 December 1962 ("Real cool alley").

The prospect behind us. First printed in *Daily Telegraph*, 12 January 1963.

Playin' my saxophone. First printed in *Daily Telegraph*, 9 February 1963 ("Dominant come-lately").

Ambassador jazz. First printed in *Daily Telegraph*, 20 March 1963 ("Ambassadors extraordinary").

The holy growl. First printed in *Daily Telegraph*, 17 April 1963 ("Legend of the jungle").

Pianists not for shooting. First printed in *Daily Telegraph*, 15 May 1963.

The end of jazz. First printed in *Daily Telegraph*, 12 June 1963 ("The death of the blues?").

Venuti and Lang. First printed in *Daily Telegraph*, 10 July 1963 ("Pieces of string").

Three-tenor fight. First printed in *Daily Telegraph*, 10 August 1963 ("Battle without conflict").

Looking at Parker. First printed in *Daily Telegraph*, 11 September 1963 ("A cool look at Bird").

Thundering herds. First printed in *Daily Telegraph*, 9 October 1963 ("The thundering herds of Woody Herman").

Snail race voluntary. First printed in *Daily Telegraph*, 30 October 1963 ("Miles without end").

Do studios kill? First printed in *Daily Telegraph*, 13 November 1963 ("Atmospheric pressure").

Ellington panorama. First printed in *Daily Telegraph*, 14 December 1963 ("As it was in the good old days").

The Billy Banks sides. First printed in *Daily Telegraph*, 11 January 1964 ("My best record of 1964").

Wandering minstrels. First printed in *Daily Telegraph*, 8 February 1964 ("Out of the hustle").

That Edwardian rag. First printed in *Daily Telegraph*, 4 March 1964 ("Mafeking relieved").

Monk. First printed in *Daily Telegraph*, 25 March 1964 ("Monk in the daylight").

New Orleans preserv'd. First printed in *Daily Telegraph*, 15 April 1964.

Decline of night-music. First printed in *Daily Telegraph*, 13 May 1964 ("Declining night music").

The new Russell. First printed in *Daily Telegraph*, 10 June 1964 ("When rocker goes mod").

All what jazz? First printed in *Daily Telegraph*, 18 July 1964 ("Shakespeare, thou art translated").

Mingus, Mingus, etc. First printed in *Daily Telegraph*, 15 August 1964 ("Mingus=Duke Minus").

How do we stand? First printed in *Daily Telegraph*, 9 September 1964 ("From clubs to concerts").

Way down yonder. First printed in *Daily Telegraph*, 7 October 1964 ("Odyssey for old-timers").

Shout it, moan it. First printed in *Daily Telegraph*, 4 November ("Shouting v. moaning").

From the festival platforms. First printed in *Daily Telegraph*, 9 December 1964 ("Memories of festivals past").

They'll none of them be missed. First printed in *Daily Telegraph*, 16 January 1965 ("Unnatural breaks").

Ask me now. First printed in *Daily Telegraph*, 15 February 1965 ("Baffling sax and baroque piano").

Some tenors. First printed in *Daily Telegraph*, 17 March 1965 ("A little night music").

The Parker legend. First printed in *Daily Telegraph*, 7 April 1965 ("Giving the Bird to the legend").

Fast and high. First printed in *Daily Telegraph*, 5 May 1965 ("So fast is so high").

Sidney Bechet from New Orleans. First printed in *Daily Telegraph*, 9 June 1965 ("Alive from New Orleans").

The tenor player with 50 legs. First printed in *Daily Telegraph*, 12 July 1965 ("Way out in all directions").

The Dixieland bag. First printed in *Daily Telegraph*, 9 August 1965 ("Dixieland rolled into one").

Idols of the twenties. First printed in *Daily Telegraph*, 15 September 1964 ("Twenties swan song").

How Billie scores. First printed in *Daily Telegraph*, 13 October 1965 ("Straight and true").

The big fellers. First printed in *Daily Telegraph*, 10 November 1965 ("Davis declaimed").

A far from indifferent guy. First printed in *Daily Telegraph*, 8 December 1965 ("The Django life").

How am I to know? First printed in *Daily Telegraph*, 9 February 1966 ("Cults and criticism").

The Bessie Smith story. First printed in *Daily Telegraph*, 9 March 1966 ("Bessie Smith alone").

Must we swallow the new wave? First printed in *Daily Telegraph*, 6 April 1966 ("The new wave smoothed out").

The documenter of jazz. First printed in *Daily Telegraph*, 4 May 1966 ("The end of a swinging era").

The bubbles Waller blew. First printed in *Daily Telegraph*, 1 June 1966 ("Fats Waller and his formula").

A loss to jazz. First printed in *Daily Telegraph*, 11 July 1966 ("Flute between two waves").

Basie: the first and best. First printed in *Daily Telegraph*, 21 September 1966 ("Basie at his best").

Can the real thing come along any more? First printed in
Daily Telegraph, 19 October 1966 ("Lloyd does something
pretty").
Goodman's guitar man. First printed in *Daily Telegraph*,
16 November 1966 ("Guitarist to Goodman").
From Clifford to Connie. First printed in *Daily Telegraph*,
5 December 1966 ("Bop-master Brown").
Credo. First printed in *Daily Telegraph*, 20 February 1967
("Purist of a sort").
The Ellington reputation. First printed in *Daily Telegraph*,
15 March 1967 ("The ducal mystique").
The funny hat men. First printed in *Daily Telegraph*,
12 April 1967 ("Funny old hat").
Ornette again. First printed in *Daily Telegraph*, 10 May 1967
("The confidence of Coleman").
The man from Defiance (Ohio). First printed in *Daily Tele-
graph*, 7 June 1967 ("Not as wild as his name").
The great Russell band. First printed in *Daily Telegraph*,
10 July 1967 ("In the front seat").
Looking back at Coltrane. Written to appear in August 1967
but, for some unknown reason, never printed.
My first name is James. First printed in *Daily Telegraph*,
27 September 1967 ("How Rushing went on singing").
Old man mainstream. First published in *Daily Telegraph*,
18 October 1967 ("In the mainstream manner").
The Panassié sides. First published in *Daily Telegraph*,
8 November 1967 ("Panassié in New Orleans").
Delving into the past. First published in *Daily Telegraph*,
6 December 1967 ("The vintage years").
'I'm coming! Beware of me!' First printed in *Daily
Telegraph*, 10 February 1968 ("Past and future
freedoms").
The hottest record ever made. First printed in *Daily Tele-
graph*, 9 March 1968 ("White-hot blues").
Home fires burning. First printed in *Daily Telegraph*, 13
April 1968 ("Blowing British").
The Dixieland band. First printed in *Daily Telegraph*,
11 May 1968 ("Dear old Dixie").
Whose flaming youth? First printed in *Daily Telegraph*,
8 June 1968 ("Nostalgia corner").

Aretha's gospel. First printed in *Daily Telegraph*, 13 July 1968.
The inimitable Jimmy Yancey. First printed in *Daily Telegraph*, 10 August 1968.
Twilight of two old gods. First printed in *Daily Telegraph*, 14 September 1968 ("Twilight of the old gods").
When they still made nice noises. First printed in *Daily Telegraph*, 12 October 1968.
How long has this been going on! First printed in *Daily Telegraph*, 9 November 1968 ("Amazing Armstrong").
Rabbit jumps the blues. First printed in *Daily Telegraph*, 14 December 1968 ("Two sides to Hodges").

Notes: Published 9 February 1970 in an edition of 4,000 copies at 35s. Some copies were remaindered in the National Book Sale, February 1974.

Reviews: K. Amis. *Daily Telegraph*, 12 February 1970, p. 6.
C. Booker. *Spectator*, CCXXIV (28 February 1970), 281–2.
S. Brown. *Listener*, LXXXIII (26 March 1970), 414, 416.
N. Bryce. *Tempo*, 93 (Summer 1970), 39.
P. Clayton. *Sunday Telegraph*, 15 February 1970, p. 17.
C. Fox. *New Statesman*, LXXIX (13 February 1970), 225–6.
C. James. *New Society*, XV (12 February 1970), 274–5.
D. Jewell. *Sunday Times*, 8 February 1970, p. 55.
D. Locke. *London Magazine*, X (June 1970), 84–6.
G. Melly. *Observer*, 8 February 1970, p. 33.
J. Wain. *Encounter*, XXXIV (May 1970), 68–71.
W. Mellers. *Musical Times*, CXI (May 1970), 507–8.

(b) First American issue   1970

All What Jazz | [long rule] | A Record Diary 1961–68 | PHILIP LARKIN | ST. MARTIN'S PRESS New York

Collation: The collation of this issue is identical with that of the English edition except for p. [vi]: '*Copyright © 1970 by Philip Larkin | All rights reserved. For information, write: | St. Martin's Press, Inc., 175 Fifth Ave., New York, N.Y. 10010 | Printed in Great Britain | Library of Congress Catalog Card Number: 74-107788 | First published in the United States of America in 1970* | [three lines]'.

Binding: Bound in strong brown (55) cloth lettered down the spine in gold: 'ALL WHAT JAZZ | [long rule] | Philip Larkin [across the foot of the spine] ST. MARTIN'S | PRESS'. Shiny white dust jacket printed in blue and black.

Paper: White wove unwatermarked paper.

Contents: As the English edition.

Notes: Published 27 July 1970 in an issue of 1,059 copies at $6.95. Out-of-print in October 1972.

Reviews: C. Clark. *Library Journal*, CXXXXV (1 October 1970), 3286.
Jazz Monthly, 183 (30 May 1970), 29.
Notes, XXVII (June 1971), 717.

A9   THE EXPLOSION   1970

THE | [rule border beginning at the top of the initial 'E' of the next word and finishing at the bottom of the same initial] EXPLOSION | [text of the poem in twenty-five lines and signature in ink 'Philip Larkin'] | [outside the rule border] The Explosion by Philip Larkin | published by Poem-of-the-Month Club Ltd, 27 Brynmaer Road, S. W. 11 | Printed by John Roberts Press Ltd. | Copyright (1970) Poem-of-the-Month Club Ltd.

Collation: 15 × 11 in. [380 × 282 mm.] Single sheet printed on one side only.

Binding: None.

Paper: White laid paper watermarked: '*Arnold* | *Signature*'.

Contents: The explosion: On the day of the explosion ... Reprinted in *Listener*, 17 August 1972, and HW.

Notes: Published in June 1970 in a signed edition of 1,000 copies available to members of the Poem-of-the-Month Club at an annual subscription of £5 5s; members were able to buy extra copies of individual poems at 65p each about a year after publication.

A10   HIGH WINDOWS   1974
(a) First edition

HIGH | WINDOWS | *by* | PHILIP LARKIN | FABER AND FABER | 3 Queen Square | London

Collation: 8½ × 5¼ in. [216 × 135 mm.] [A]–C⁸, pp. [i–ii, 1–6] 7 [8] 9–42 [43–46].

[i–ii]: laid down as front endpaper. [1–2]: blank. [3]: half title. [4]: 'by the same author | [star] | [three lines] | [star] | [one line]'. [5]: title page. [6]: '*First published in 1974 | by Faber and Faber Limited | 3 Queen Square London W C 1 | Printed in Great Britain by | The Bowering Press Limited Plymouth | All rights reserved* | ISBN 0 571 10552 1 | © *1974 by Philip Larkin*'. 7: contents. [8]: textual note. 9–42: text. [43–44]: blank. [45–46]: laid down as rear endpaper.

Binding: Bound in light-grey (264) cloth lettered down the spine in gold: '*High Windows* [dot] *Philip Larkin* [dot] *Faber*'. White shiny dust jacket printed in grey and medium greenish blue. The second impression is bound in yellow-grey (93) cloth.

Paper: White wove unwatermarked paper.

Contents: To the sea: To step over the low wall that divides . . . First printed in *London Magazine*, January 1970, and reprinted in *Antaeus*, Winter 1973.

Sympathy in White major: When I drop four cubes of ice . . . First printed in *London Magazine*, December 1967.

The trees: The trees are coming into leaf . . . First printed in *New Statesman*, 17 May 1968, and reprinted in *Humberside*, Autumn 1971, and *Antaeus*, Winter 1973.

Livings: I deal with farmers, things like dips and feed . . . First printed in *Observer*, 20 February 1972.

Forget what did: Stopping the diary . . .

High windows: When I see a couple of kids . . .

Friday night in the Royal Station hotel: Light spreads darkly downwards from the high . . . First printed in the *Morning Telegraph* [Sheffield], 7 January 1967, and reprinted in *Humberside*, Autumn 1968.

The old fools: What do they think has happened, the old fools . . . First printed in *Listener*, 1 February 1973.

Going, going: I thought it would last my time . . . First printed in *How do you want to live?* ("Prologue") and *Observer*, 4 June 1972, and revised here.

The card-players: Jan van Hogspeuw staggers to the door . . . First printed in *Encounter*, October 1970.

The building: Higher than the handsomest hotel . . . First printed in *New Statesman*, 17 March 1972.

Posterity: Jake Balowsky, my biographer . . . First pri
New Statesman, 28 June 1968.
Dublinesque: Down stucco sidestreets . . . First print
Encounter, October 1970.
Homage to a government: Next year we are to bring the
soldiers home . . . First printed in *Sunday Times*, 19 January
1969.
This be the verse: They fuck you up, your mum and
dad . . .
How distant: How distant, the departures of young men . . .
First printed in *Listener*, 26 October 1967.
Sad steps: Groping back to bed after a piss . . . First printed
in *New Statesman*, 28 June 1968.
Solar: Suspended lion face . . . First printed in *Queen*, 25
May 1966.
Annus mirabilis: Sexual intercourse began . . . First printed
in *Cover* [Oxford], February 1968, and reprinted in *London
Magazine*, January 1970, and *Michigan Quarterly Review*,
Summer 1970.
Vers de société: *My wife and I have asked a crowd of craps* . . .
First printed in *New Statesman*, 18 June 1971.
Show Saturday: Grey day for the Show, but cars jam the
narrow lanes . . . First printed in *Encounter*, February 1974.
Money: Quarterly, is it, money reproaches me . . .
Cut grass: Cut grass lies frail . . . First printed in *Listener*,
29 July 1971.
The explosion: On the day of the explosion . . . First printed
as a broadside (1970) and reprinted in *Listener*, 17 August
1972.

Notes: Published 3 June 1974 in an impression of 6,000 copies at
£1.40, and reprinted in September 1974 (7,500 copies) and January
1975 (6,000 copies).

Reviews: K. Amis. *Observer*, 2 June 1974, p. 32.
J. Bayley. *Times Literary Supplement*, 21 June 1974, pp. 653–5.
D. Bowman. *Akros*, x (April 1976), 77–82.
A. Brownjohn. *New Statesman*, LXXXVII (14 June 1974),
854 and 856.
C. B. Cox. *Sunday Telegraph*, 16 June 1974, p. 15.
T. Eagleton, *Tablet*, 29 June 1974, p. 625.

P. Gardner. *Phoenix*, 13 (Spring 1975), 94–100.
D. Graham. *Stand*, XVI ([March] 1975), 76.
G. Hartley. *Phoenix*, 13 (Spring 1975), 87–92.
C. James. *Encounter*, XLII (June 1974), 65–71.
E. Jennings. *Daily Telegraph*, 13 June 1974, p. 10.
D. May. *Guardian*, 6 June 1974, p. 11.
R. Nye. *The Times*, 6 June 1974, p. 8.
J. Wain. *Oxford Literary Review*, Summer 1974, pp. 2–3.

(b) First American edition
1974

HIGH│WINDOWS│PHILIP LARKIN│[device: three fishes]│FARRAR, STRAUS AND GIROUX│NEW YORK

Collation: 8 × 5⅜ in. [203 × 140 mm.] [1–3]⁸, pp. [i–iv, 1–8] 9–42 [43–44]. The paperback issue measures 7⅞ × 5¼ in. [200 × 136 mm.].
[i–ii]: blank. [iii]: half title. [iv]: blank. [1]: title page. [2]: '© 1974 by Philip Larkin│First American printing, 1974│All rights reserved│Printed in the United States of America│[five lines]'. [3]: textual note. [4]: blank. [5]: contents. [6]: blank. [7]: '*High Windows*'. [8]: blank. 9–42: text. [43–44]: blank.

Binding: Bound in blackish-blue (188) cloth lettered down the spine in gold: '*High Windows Larkin Farrar* [dot] *Straus* [dot] *Giroux*'. White shiny dust jacket printed in medium blue and black.

The paperback issue is glued in a white card cover lettered down the spine: '[in black] *HIGH WINDOWS*│*PHILIP LARKIN* [in blue] *N490*'; and across the front cover: '[in white on a blue panel] *High*│*Windows*│[in black] *Philip*│*Larkin*│[in blue] *NOONDAY 490* $2.95'. The rear cover carries reviews of the English edition and previous books.

Paper: White wove unwatermarked paper.

Contents: As the English edition.

Notes: Published 3 December 1974 at $6.95 for the hardback issue; the paperback issue was published on 1 October 1975 at $2.95. The publisher prefers not to reveal the number of copies printed, but the hardback issue was reprinted late in 1976.

Reviews: C. Bedient. *New York Times*, 12 January 1975, section 7, p. 3.
Choice, XII (June 1975), 534.
S. S. Hilliard. *Prairie Schooner*, XLIX (Fall 1975), 270–1.

R. Murphy. *New York Review of Books*, XXII (15 May 1975), 30–3.

S. Poss. *Western Humanities Review*, XXIX (Autumn 1975), 398–402.

W. H. Pritchard. *Hudson Review*, XXVIII (Summer 1975), 302–8.

Virginia Quarterly Review, LII (Spring 1976), 50.

B

WORKS EDITED OR WITH
CONTRIBUTIONS
BY
PHILIP LARKIN

B1   OXFORD POETRY 1942–1943   1943

OXFORD | POETRY | 1942–1943 | Edited   by   IAN   DAVIE | OXFORD ·
BASIL BLACKWELL | MDCCCCXLIII

Collation: 7½ × 5 in. [190 × 126 mm.] [A]–D⁸, [1–2] 3–64. [1]: title page.
[2]: 'Printed in Great Britain for BASIL BLACKWELL & MOTT
LIMITED | by A. R. MOWBRAY & CO. LIMITED, London and
Oxford'. 3: contributors. 4: note on the compilation. 5–64: text.

Binding: Glued in a stiff very dark greenish-blue (175) card cover with a
white paper label stuck on the upper-left front cover lettered across in
black: 'OXFORD | POETRY | 1942–1943 | OXFORD | BASIL BLACKWELL'.
Edges untrimmed.

Paper: Cream wove unwatermarked paper.

Contents: A stone church damaged by a bomb: Planted deeper than
        roots . . . p. 41.
        Mythological introduction: A white girl lay on the grass . . .
        p. 42. First printed in *Arabesque*, Hilary term 1943.
        Poem: I dreamed of an outstretched arm of land . . . p. 43.
        First printed in *Arabesque*, Hilary term 1943, and reprinted in
        NS.

Notes: Published 12 June 1943 in an edition of 500 copies at 3s. 6d.
Larkin was invited to contribute by the editor.

B2   POETRY FROM OXFORD IN WARTIME   1945

"*Go, for they call you, Shepherd.*" | [long rule] | POETRY FROM | OXFORD |
IN WARTIME | Edited by | WILLIAM BELL | THE FORTUNE PRESS
| 79 BUCKINGHAM PALACE ROAD | LONDON

Collation: 7¼ × 5 in. [188 × 124 mm.] [A]–F⁸, pp. [1–2] 3–93 [94–96].
[1]: title page. [2]: 'FIRST PUBLISHED IN 1945'. 3–6: contents.
7: quotation from Dryden. 8–[94]: text. [95–96]: advertisements for
the Fortune Press.

Binding: Bound in smooth dark purplish-blue cloth (201) lettered up
the spine in gold: '*POETRY FROM OXFORD IN WARTIME*'.
Top edge only cut. A later issue is bound in grained, dark purplish-
blue (201) cloth. White dust jacket printed in dark blue.

Paper: White laid paper watermarked: '[a crown] | Glastonbury', with a long 's'.

Contents: I see a girl dragged by the wrists . . . pp. 72–3.
> Love, we must part now; do not let it be . . . p. 73.
> The bottle is drunk out by one . . . p. 74.
> Heaviest of flowers, the head . . . p. 74.
> The horns of the morning . . . p. 75.
> All catches alight . . . pp. 75–6.
> The moon is full tonight . . . p. 76.
> I put my mouth . . . p. 77.
> So through that unripe day you bore your head . . . p. 77.
> Morning has spread again . . . p. 78.
> All reprinted in NS.

Notes: Published in February 1945 (*Whitaker's Four Year Cumulative Book-list, 1944–1947*) at 6s. The printer, J. Looker Ltd. of Poole in Dorset, unfortunately has no record of the number of copies printed, but it is unlikely that more than 500 copies were produced.

B3   POETS OF THE 1950's   1956

POETS OF THE 1950's | AN ANTHOLOGY OF NEW | ENGLISH VERSE |
Edited, with an Introduction, | *by* | D. J. ENRIGHT | TOKYO | KEN-
KYUSHA LTD. | 1955

Collation: $7\frac{5}{16} \times 5$ in. [183 × 127 mm.] [1–15]⁴ [16]², pp. [i–ii] iii–v
[vi], 1–116 [117–118].
[i]: title page. [ii]: '*First published in Japan 1955* | [nine lines] | [rule] |
Printed by THE KENKYUSHA PRESS, *Tokyo.* | *Made in Japan.*' iii–v:
contents. [vi]: blank. 1–116: text. [117]: colophon. [118]: blank.

Binding: Bound in smoothish, dark grey-red (20) cloth lettered across
the spine in gold: '[thick/thin rule] | POETS | OF THE | 1950's | [short
rule] | Ed. by D. J. | ENRIGHT | [thin/thick rule] | KENKYUSHA'. Pale-
pink dust jacket printed in light brown.

Paper: White wove unwatermarked paper.

Contents: [A note on poetry and his writing it.] pp. 77–8.
> Skin: Obedient daily dress . . . p. 79.
> Maiden name: Marrying left your maiden name disused . . .
> p. 80.

Less deceived: Even so distant, I can taste the grief . . . p. 81.
Wedding-wind: The wind blew all my wedding day . . .
p. 82.
At grass: The eye can hardly pick them out . . . pp. 83–4.
Next, please: Always too eager for the future, we . . . pp.
85–6.
If, my darling: If my darling were once to decide . . .
pp. 87–8.
Going: There is an evening coming in . . . p. 89.
All reprinted from TLD, except the prefatory note.

Notes: Published 14 January 1956 in an impression of 2,000 copies at
¥150 and reprinted in 1958 (1,000 copies). The dust jacket of the first
impression misprints Larkin's name as "Larkins". The note on pp. 77–8
was not intended for publication.

B4   NEW POEMS 1958   1958

New Poems | [ornamental rule enclosing the date: '1958'] | *Edited by* |
BONAMY DOBRÉE | LOUIS MACNEICE | PHILIP LARKIN | [device:
mermaid with trumpet shell within an oval rule] | *London* | MICHAEL
JOSEPH

Collation: 7⅞ × 5⅛ in. [200 × 132 mm.] [A]–H⁸, pp. [1–9] 10 [11–12]
13–113 [114–115] 116–123 [124–128]. The last leaf is laid down as an
endpaper.
[1]: half title. [2]: blank. [3]: title page. [4]: '*First published by* |
MICHAEL JOSEPH LTD | *26 Bloomsbury Street* | *London W.C.I* | *1958* |
© *copyright 1958 by the P.E.N.* | *Set and printed in Great Britain by*
Unwin Brothers Ltd. at the | *Gresham Press, Woking, in Bembo type,*
eleven point, leaded, on | *paper made by Henry Bruce at Currie, Midlothian,*
and bound by | *James Burn at Esher*'. [5–7]: contents. [8]: blank. [9]–10:
introduction [signed] 'B. D. | P.A.L. | L. MacN.', and acknowledge-
ments. [11]: '*The Poems*'. [12]: blank. 13–113: text. [114]: blank.
[115]–123: notes on contributors. [124–126]: blank. [127–128]: endpaper laid down.

Binding: Quarter bound in vivid red (12) cloth lettered across the spine
in white: '*New* | *Poems* | [ornamental swelled rule] | *1958* | [ornamental
swelled rule] | *a* | *P.E.N.* | *Anthology* | [device] | MICHAEL JOSEPH', with

the boards covered in white paper printed in a repeat pattern in reddish brown, olive green and grey. All edges trimmed. Grey dust jacket printed in reddish brown.

Paper: As above; white wove unwatermarked.

Contents: Introduction. pp. 9–10.

Notes: Published 10 November 1958 in an impression of 2,116 copies at 13s. 6d. and out of print in August 1962. The Autumn choice of the Poetry Book Society Ltd., and the seventh volume in this particular P.E.N. anthology series. The initial invitation was dated 9 August 1957 and the editors held their first meeting on 28 September 1957. Most of the editorial work was carried out by Dobrée and Larkin and was completed by 15 April 1958. The introduction was drafted by Larkin and Dobrée.

B5   POETRY 1960   1960

[wrapper title] A CRITICAL QUARTERLY SUPPLEMENT | [blue rule] | [fancy shaded] POETRY | [in blue] *An anthology of the best poems* | [fancy shaded] 1960 | [in blue] *by new writers in the '50s: new poems* | [fancy shaded] An Appetiser | [in blue] *by established poets: prize poems* | [blue rule] | [names of 18 poets in nine double-columned lines] | PRICE ONE SHILLING

Collation: $8\frac{5}{8} \times 5\frac{1}{2}$ in. [219×141 mm.] One unsigned gathering of 24 leaves, pp. [1–2] 3–24.
[outer front wrapper]: title page. [inner front wrapper]: acknowledgements. [1]: contents. [2]: introduction [signed] 'C. B. Cox | A. E. Dyson'. [3]–22: text. 23: subscription form for *The Critical Quarterly*. 24: subscription form for more copies of this publication. [inner rear wrapper]: details of *The Critical Quarterly*. [outer rear wrapper]: advertisement for *The Critical Quarterly*.

Binding: Stapled twice in a light bluish-grey (190) card cover.

Paper: White wove unwatermarked paper.

Contents: At grass: The eye can hardly pick them out . . . p. 3.
          Reprinted from TLD.
          Love songs in age: She kept her songs, they took so little space . . . p. 16. Reprinted in TWW.

Notes: Probably published 1 February 1960 in an edition of 12,000 copies at 1s. Out of print in January 1962 (*Critical Quarterly*, IV (Spring 1962), 3).

B6   POET'S CHOICE   1962

POET'S | CHOICE | [ornamental rule] | EDITED BY | Paul Engle and Joseph Langland | [device: winged cherub riding a rampant lion] | THE DIAL PRESS NEW YORK 1962
Collation: 9⅛×6⅛ in. [231×152 mm.] [1–8]¹⁶ [9]⁴ [10–11]¹⁶, pp. [2, i–iii] iv–xvii [xviii–xx], 1–303 [304–306].
[*2*]: blanks. [i]: half title. [ii]: blank. [iii]: title page. [iv]: '*Copyright ©
1962 by Paul Engle and Joseph Langland* | ALL RIGHTS RESERVED |
Library of Congress Catalog Card Number: 62–17684 | DESIGNED BY
ALAN M. HEICKLEN | MANUFACTURED IN THE UNITED STATES OF
AMERICA | BY THE HADDON CRAFTSMEN, SCRANTON, PA. | [fifty-
one lines of acknowledgements]'. v–vii: acknowledgements. [viii]:
blank. ix–xi: contents. [xii]: blank. xiii–xvii: introduction. [xviii]:
blank. [xix]: 'POET'S | CHOICE | [short ornamental rule]'. [xx]: blank.
1–303: text. [304–306]: blank.

Binding: Bound in rough dark-red (16) cloth lettered across the spine in gold: '[ornament] | [title down the spine] POET'S CHOICE | [orna-
ment] | EDITED BY | ENGLE | AND | LANGLAND [the 'G' is fancy with a tail flourish] | [device] | DIAL'. Top edge only cut; orange-red end-
papers. Smooth cream dust jacket printed in red, black and gold.

Paper: White wove unwatermarked paper.

Contents: Philip Larkin. pp. 202–203.
        Absences: Rain patters on a sea that tilts and sighs . . . with
        explanatory note and facsimile signature. The poem is
        reprinted from TLD.

Notes: Published 29 October 1962 in an edition of 10,000 copies at $6,
raised to $6.95 in December 1962 and still in print at the end of 1974.
Another edition was issued in 1966 by Time Inc. as one of the books
in the "Time Reading Program", and a paperback edition was published by the Dell Publishing Company in January 1966 at $1.95 as a
Delta Book.

B7   "POETRY IN THE MAKING"   1967

CATALOGUE OF AN EXHIBITION|OF POETRY MANUSCRIPTS IN|
THE BRITISH MUSEUM|April–June 1967|by|JENNY LEWIS|with
contributions by|C. DAY LEWIS|T. C. SKEAT|PHILIP LARKIN|
Published by TURRET BOOKS for|THE ARTS COUNCIL OF GREAT
BRITAIN & |THE BRITISH MUSEUM

Collation: 9×5¾ in. [238×150 mm.] [1–3]⁸[4]¹⁰, pp. [1–8] 9–22 [23–24]
25–68. Four plates are tipped in between pp. 32 and 33.
[1]: half title [2]: blank. [3]: title page. [4]: 'Published in 1967 by Turret
Books, 5 Kensington Church Walk, |W8|[four lines]|Printed by
Villiers Publications Ltd, Ingestre Road, London NW5'. [5]: contents.
[6]: acknowledgements. [7]: list of illustrations. [8]: blank. 9–10:
preface, by C. Day Lewis. 11–13: introduction, by T. C. Skeat. 14–21:
Operation manuscript, by Philip Larkin. 22: membership of the
Arts Council's Poetry Manuscripts Committee 1967. [23]: 'CATA-
LOGUE OF|THE EXHIBITION|[three lines in italic]'. [24]: blank.
25–68: text. [60]: blank. 61–67: index to the collection. 68: erratum.

Signed and lettered copies carry the following additional statement
on p. [4] before the printer's imprint: 'One hundred and twenty-six
copies of this catalogue have been|signed by the authors concerned.
One hundred of these are|numbered from 1 to 100, and twenty-six
are lettered from A to Z.|[followed by the copy number and the
signatures of Day Lewis, Larkin, Skeat and Lewis in four lines]'.

Binding: Bound in medium-green (145) cloth lettered down the spine
in gold: 'Poetry in the Making'. All edges trimmed with medium
greenish-yellow endpapers. White dust wrapper printed in medium
yellowish green and dark olive green.

Signed and lettered copies are bound in smooth dark purplish-blue
(201) buckram with light purplish-blue endpapers; copies issued in
wrappers are glued in a white card cover lettered down the spine in
dark olive green: 'Poetry in the Making'; and in white across the front
cover on a medium yellowish-green panel across the top third of the
cover: 'Poetry in the Making'. The bottom two-thirds of the wrapper
are dark olive green. The rear wrapper carries the price: '12/6'.

Paper: Cream laid paper watermarked: '[a crown]|Glastonbury',
with a long 's'.

Contents: Operation manuscript. pp. 14–21.

Notes: Published in April 1967 in an edition of 2,126 copies, 126 of which were numbered and lettered copies (the lettered copies being mainly for the authors), 500 of which were issued bound, and 1,500 in soft covers. The bound copies were priced at 25s. and those in soft covers 12s. 6d.

B8   VERNON WATKINS, 1906–1967   1970

Vernon Watkins | 1906–1967 | [swelled rule] | *edited by* | LESLIE NORRIS | FABER AND FABER | London

Collation: 8½×5⅜ in. [211×137 mm.] [A–G]⁸, pp. [1–6] 7 [8] 9–11 [12] 13–68 [69] 70–105 [106–112]. The last leaf is laid down as an endpaper. [1–2]: blanks. [3]: half title. [4]: blank. [5]: title page. [6]: '*First published in 1970 | by Faber and Faber Limited | 24 Russell Square London WC1 | Printed in Great Britain | by Ebenezer Baylis and Son, Limited | The Trinity Press, Worcester, and London | All rights reserved* | SBN 571 08904 6 | This collection © Faber and Faber Ltd. 1970'. 7: acknowledgements. [8]: blank. 9–10: contents. 11: illustrations. [12]: blank. 13–14: introduction. 15–105: text. [106–110]: blank. [111–112]: endpaper laid down.

Binding: Bound in light reddish-brown (42) cloth lettered down the spine in gold: 'Vernon Watkins 1906–1967 [rule across] EDITED BY | LESLIE NORRIS [across the spine] Faber'. All edges trimmed. White dust wrapper printed in blue, light yellowish green and light grey yellowish brown.

Paper: White wove unwatermarked paper.

Contents: Vernon Watkins: an encounter and a re-encounter. pp. 28–33. First printed in *Mabon*, Spring 1969.

Notes: First published 9 February 1970 in an edition of 1,570 copies at 36s.

B9   JOHN BETJEMAN: COLLECTED POEMS   1971

JOHN BETJEMAN | *Collected* | *Poems* | ENLARGED EDITION | Compiled by The Earl of Birkenhead | *Introduction by Philip Larkin* | [ornament: two bells] | 1971 | HOUGHTON MIFFLIN COMPANY | BOSTON

Collation: 7¼×4½ in. [183×110 mm.] [1–13]¹⁶, pp. [i–iv] v [vi] vii–xv

[xvi] xvii–xli [xlii–xliv], 1–366 [367–372]. [i]: half title. [ii]: blank. [iii]: title page. [iv]: 'First Printing A | [two lines] | Introduction copyright © 1971 by Philip Larkin | [five lines] | I.S.B.N.: 0-395-12705-X | Library of Congress Catalog Card Number: 77–162003 | Printed in the United States of America'. v: acknowledgements. [vi]: blank. vii–xv: contents. [xvi]: blank. xvii–xli: introduction [signed] PHILIP LARKIN | Hull, England | May, 1971 | [two lines]'. [xlii]: blank. [xliii]: 'Collected | Poems'. [xliv]: blank. 1–366: text. [367–372]: blank.

Binding: Bound in light yellowish-green (119) cloth lettered down the spine in gold on two deep yellowish-green panels: 'Collected Poems BETJEMAN [across the spine on the cloth] hmco'; and across the front cover: '[in green on the cloth] JOHN BETJEMAN | [in gold on a deep yellowish-green panel] Collected | Poems | [ornament: two bells]'. Top edge stained deep yellowish green. White dust wrapper printed in yellow, blue, green and black.

Paper: White wove unwatermarked paper.

Contents: Introduction. pp. xvii–xli. Reprinted in slightly revised form in the *Cornhill,* Autumn 1971.

Notes: First published 28 September 1971 in an edition of 4,000 copies at $7.50.

B10   HOW DO YOU WANT TO LIVE?   1972

[all across a photograph of Glantees farm, Newton-on-the-moor] How do you want to live? | A Report on the human Habitat | Presented in January 1972 to | THE SECRETARY OF STATE FOR THE ENVIRONMENT | THE RIGHT HONOURABLE PETER WALKER MBE MP | *A study of public opinion, undertaken at his request | in connection with the United Nations Conference on the Human | Environment, Stockholm, June 1972 |* LONDON HER MAJESTY'S STATIONERY OFFICE 1972

Collation: 8¼ × 5¾ in. [210 × 147 mm.] A⁸B¹⁰[C]–O⁸, pp. [i–iii] iv–ix [x–xi] xii, 1–214 [215–216]. B2 is signed 'B*'. [i]: blank. [ii–iii]: title pages. iv: '© *Crown copyright 1972* | Published for the Department of the Environment | SBN 11 750514 5'. v: foreword. vi: list of photographs otherwise uncaptioned. vii: contents. viii: blank. ix: letter of transmission signed by members. [x–xi]:

'Prologue [poem signed] PHILIP LARKIN'. xii: blank. 1–214: text. [215]: blank. [216]: list of government bookshops, etc.

Binding: Glued in a white card cover lettered down the spine in black: 'HOW DO YOU WANT TO LIVE? HMSO'; and across the front cover in white, on a photograph by Lord Snowdon of a naiad (Undine?) emerging from a pool: 'HUMAN HABITAT: | HOW DO YOU | WANT TO LIVE?'.

Paper: Shiny white unwatermarked paper.

Contents: Prologue: I thought it would last my time . . . pp. [x–xi]. Specially written for the report, this version was modified at the request of the chairman, the Countess of Dartmouth (*Private Eye*, 274 (16 June 1972), p. 6), and reprinted in the *Observer*, 4 June 1972; the unmodified version is reprinted in HW ("Going, going").

Notes: Published 24 May 1972 in an impression of 6,490 copies at £1.80 and reprinted in August 1972 (3,720 copies).

B11 ANTIQUARIAN BOOK FAIR 1972 1972

[wrapper title] Europa Hotel Grosvenor Square W 1 | 13th 14th 15th June. 11–8 daily | [within a black rule border a woodcut of pressmen working an old hand press] | [in white] Antiquarian Book Fair | 1972

Collation: 8⅛×11⅝ in. [207×295 mm.] single sheet folding twice to 8⅛×3⅛ in. [207×98 mm.] with an unpaged six-leaf catalogue of bookseller exhibitors stapled twice in the first fold.

Binding: None.

Paper: The wrapper is of white wove unwatermarked card; the list of booksellers on dark orange-yellow unwatermarked paper.

Contents: Introduction. [Inside front and middle wrapper.]

Notes: Published 13 June 1972 in an edition of 5,000 copies for free distribution to visitors; printed by Robert Stockwell Ltd. The Book Fair was actually opened by Tom Stoppard at 11.15 a.m. on 13 June 1972.

B12   THE OXFORD BOOK OF   1973
          TWENTIETH-CENTURY ENGLISH VERSE

The Oxford Book of | Twentieth-Century | English Verse | Chosen by |
Philip Larkin | Clarendon Press · Oxford | 1973

Collation: 8½× 5 in. [215× 130 mm.] [1–20]¹⁶[21]¹²[22]¹⁶, pp. [2, i–iv]
v–xix [xx] xxi–l, 1–625 [626] 627–641 [642–644].

[2]: blanks. [i]: half title. [ii]: blank. [iii]: title page. [iv]: '[five lines] |
© OXFORD UNIVERSITY PRESS 1973 | PRINTED IN GREAT BRITAIN
BY | RICHARD CLAY (THE CHAUCER PRESS), LTD. | BUNGAY,
SUFFOLK'. v–vi: preface. vii–xix: acknowledgements. [xx]: blank.
xxi–l: contents. 1–625: text. [626]: blank. 627–38: index of first lines.
639–641: index of authors. [642–644]: blank.
The second impression adds to p. [iv] a statement on photocopying,
the ISBN number 0 19 812137 7 and drops the date 1973 from the
title page. Pages 386–388 and 579–583 are reset to allow fuller versions
of "Aubade" by Empson and "The Byrnies" by Gunn.

Binding: Bound in smooth, deep purplish-blue (197) cloth lettered
across the spine in gold: '[all within a gold ornament border] The |
Oxford | Book of | Twentieth | Century | English | Verse | [device]', and
across the front cover: '[all within a blind stamped ornamental border]
THE | OXFORD BOOK OF | TWENTIETH | CENTURY | ENGLISH VERSE'.
All edges trimmed. Shiny white dust wrapper printed in red and olive
green.
   The dust wrapper of the American issue is printed in yellow, light
blue and black and is of a different design from the English edition.
   The first Readers Union issue for the Arts Book Society is bound in
blackish-purple (230) cloth patterned paper boards, and lettered as the
first edition with the substitution of the following for the arms of the
University device on the spine: '[all within a rectangular wide rule
border] ARTS BOOK | SOCIETY'. The dust wrapper has a similar substi-
tution within a rectangular three rule border. The second Readers
Union issue is of the third impression and the binding is the same as
that for the Arts Book Society issue, except that for the arms of the
University device is substituted that of the Readers Union, a spreading
tree with roots and the letters RU within an oval rule border; this
substitution is also made on the dust wrapper. The fourth printing has

a newly designed dust wrapper with a reproduction of a mural by Stanley Spencer in the Sandham Memorial chapel at Burghclere.

Paper: White wove unwatermarked paper.

Contents: Preface. pp. v–vi.

Notes: Published 29 March 1973 in an impression of 29,300 copies at £3. Of this first printing 5,500 copies were supplied for the first American issue in June 1973 and 3,000 copies were supplied to the Readers Union for its issue. The title was reprinted in June 1973 (13,550 copies; of which 2,500 copies were supplied in January 1974 for the United States), February 1974 (20,000 copies; of which 2,500 copies were supplied in June 1974 for the United States, and 3,000 copies were supplied to the Readers Union), and February 1975 (15,000 copies).

A Braille edition for blind readers was produced by the Royal National Institute for the Blind in 1975.

Reviews: W. H. Auden. *Guardian*, 29 March 1973, p. 16.
C. Bedient. *New York Times*, 17 June 1973, section 7, p. 4.
B. Bergonzi. *Prospice*, 1 ([December] 1973), 44–7.
R. L. Brett. *Humberside*, xvii (Autumn 1973), 9–11.
C. Connolly. *Sunday Times*, 1 April 1973, p. 35.
D. Davie. *Listener*, lxxxix (29 March 1973), 420–1.
D. Donoghue. *New York Review of Books*, xx (26 April 1973), 26.
N. Dennis. *Sunday Telegraph*, 1 April 1973, p. 12.
I. Hamilton. *New Statesman*, lxxxv (30 March 1973), 463.
R. Lowell. *Encounter*, xl (May 1973), 66–8.
P. Scupham. *Phoenix*, 11–12 (Autumn/Winter 1973/4) 173–82.
L. E. Sissman. *New Yorker*, xlviiii (8 June 1973) 110.
C. P. Snow. *Financial Times*, 29 March 1973, p. 37.
S. Spender. *Spectator*, ccxxx (31 March 1973), 394–5.
The Times, 27 April 1973, p. 18.
Times Literary Supplement, 13 April 1973, pp. 405–7.

B13   LET THE POET CHOOSE   1973

[in olive green] *Let the* | *Poet Choose* | edited by | JAMES GIBSON | [device: flying horse within a double rule circular border] | HARRAP LONDON

Collation: 8½×5⅜ in. [216×136 mm.] [1–12]⁸, pp. [1–4] 5 [6] 7 [8] 9–15 [16] 17–191 [192].

[1]: half title. [2]: blank. [3]: title page. [4]: 'First published in Great Britain 1973 | by GEORGE C. HARRAP & CO. LTD | 182–184 High Holborn, London, W.C.1V 7AX | © James Gibson 1973 | [three lines] | ISBN 0 245 51932 7 (boards) | 0 245 51934 3 (limp) | Printed in Great Britain by | WESTERN PRINTING SERVICES LTD, BRISTOL'. 5: 'THE POETS | [names of 44 poets in double column]'. [6]: blank. 7: preface. [8]: blank. 9–10: acknowledgements. 11–15: contents. 17–191: text. [192]: blank. The whole book is printed in olive green.

Binding: Bound in vivid orange (48) paper Linson boards lettered down the spine in olive green: 'LET THE POET CHOOSE JAMES GIBSON HARRAP'. All edges trimmed. White dust wrapper printed in dark brown and strong orange yellow.

Some copies are glued in white paper wrappers printed in dark brown and lettered down the spine in white: 'Gibson Let the Poet Choose [device]'. The front cover is lettered in white: '[within a curved panel of a thin white and thick yellow rule] edited by James Gibson | [within a circular panel of a thin white rule and thick yellow rule] Let | the Poet | Choose | [facsimile signatures of the poets in yellow within a square panel of similar white and yellow rules]'. The rear wrapper repeats the design with supplementary information.

Paper: White wove unwatermarked paper.

Contents: Philip Larkin [prefatory note]. p. 102.
MCMXIV: Those long uneven lines ... pp. 102–3.
Send no money: Standing under the fobbed ... p.104.
Both poems reprinted from TWW.

Notes: Published 14 May 1973 in an edition of 12,000 copies, of which 10,000 were issued in boards at £1.70 and 2,000 were issued in limp covers at 80p.

B14   A KEEPSAKE   1973

[in red] *A Keepsake* | [in black] *from the New Library* | [ornament in red] | at the | School of Oriental & African Studies | *5 October 1973*

Collation: 8½×6¼ in. [216×163 mm.] One unsigned gathering of six leaves.

[1]: title page. [2]: '© 1973 by the contributors'. [3]: epigraphs. [4]: blank. [5-11]: texts. [12]: 'One thousand one hundred copies | were privately published for the Librarian | of the School of Oriental and African Studies, | University of London, | by Mansell Information/ Publishing Limited | for free distribution to guests | at the School on 5 October 1973. | Designed by Frances Ross Duncan. | Hand set in Caslon's *English* type, | cast in William Caslon's matrices of 1732, | and printed at the John Roberts Press | on Sabines Small Rape mould-made paper.'

Binding: Stitched twice in a white card cover round which is glued a dark greyish-yellow (91) Ingres Fabriano wrapper lettered across the front: '[in red] *A Keepsake* | [in black] *from the New Library* | at the School of Oriental & African Studies | *5 October 1973*'.
Paper: See above.

Contents: Continuing to live: Continuing to live—that is, repeat . . . p. [9].
The misprint 'is' for 'it' in line 18 is corrected by hand in ink in most copies.

Notes: The circumstances of publication are outlined above.

B15   THE ARTS COUNCIL COLLECTION OF   1974
MODERN LITERARY MANUSCRIPTS, 1963-1972

THE ARTS COUNCIL | COLLECTION OF | MODERN LITERARY | MANU-SCRIPTS | 1963-1972 | A CATALOGUE BY | JENNY STRATFORD | WITH A PREFACE BY | PHILIP LARKIN | [device: a castle with three turrets, one with a flag carrying the letter 'T'] | TURRET BOOKS | 1974

Collation: 9¼ × 5⅞ in. [235 × 150 mm.] [1]¹²[2-10]⁸[11]¹², pp. [i-v] vi-ix [x] xi-xix [xx] xxi-xxiii [xxiv], 1-168.
[i]: half title. [ii]: 'BY THE SAME AUTHOR | [one line]'. [iii]: title page. [iv]: 'Published in 1974 by TURRET BOOKS | 1b, 1c & 1d Kensington Church Walk, | London W8 4NB | [three lines] | Printed by Villiers Publications Ltd. | Ingestre Road, London NW 5'. [v]: contents. vi: illustrations. vii-ix: acknowledgements. [x]: blank. xi-xii: preface. xiii-xix: introduction. [xx]: blank. xxi-xxii: appendix. xxiii: table of manuscripts acquired 1963-1972. [xxiv]: blank. 1-159: text with 16

pages of plates tipped in between pp. 80 and 81. [160]: blank. 161–168: index.

Binding: Bound in deep purplish-blue (197) bubbled cloth lettered down the spine in gold: 'Catalogue of Modern Literary Manuscripts Stratford'. White dust wrapper printed in deep blue, deep purplish blue and black.

Paper: Cream wove unwatermarked paper.

Contents: Preface [signed] PHILIP LARKIN. pp. xi–xii.
        Anthony Thwaite [:description of manuscripts] pp. 115–17.
        Stevie Smith [:description of manuscripts] pp. 158–159.

Notes: Published July 1974 in an edition of 1,500 copies at £6.

B16   POETRY SUPPLEMENT   1974

Poetry Supplement | COMPILED BY | PHILIP LARKIN | FOR THE | POETRY BOOK | SOCIETY | *CHRISTMAS* | 1974

Collation: 8 × 5⅛ in. [203 × 129 mm.] [1–3]⁸, pp. [1–48].
[1]: title page. [2]: blank. [3–42]: text. [43–46]: notes on contributors. [47]: blank. [48]: '*Printed by the John Roberts Press | and published by the Poetry Book Society at 105 Piccadilly, London, W1V 0AU*'.

Binding: Glued in a light grey-red (18) wrapper lettered across the front cover: '[device, fancy letters 'P | B S' in a laurel wreath within a square blue rule border] | [in black] POETRY | SUPPLEMENT | [in blue] COMPILED BY | [in black] PHILIP LARKIN | [in blue] for the POETRY | BOOK SOCIETY | [in black] CHRISTMAS '74'; and on the rear cover in the lower left corner: '40p'.

Paper: White wove unwatermarked paper.

Contents: The life with a hole in it: When I throw back my head and howl . . . p. [25].

Notes: Published 1 December 1974 in an edition of 2,500 copies, of which 2,000 copies were distributed free to members of the Poetry Book Society and the remaining 500 copies were put on sale at 40p.

B17   ADVENTURES WITH THE IRISH BRIGADE   1975

[title underlined once] ADVENTURES|WITH|THE IRISH BRIGADE|
TO THE INFANTRY|Who, as they grovelled and prayed in|the ditch,
touched the hand of GOD.

Collation: 7⅞×6½ in. [200×165 mm.] 95 single leaves, pp. [i–viii],
1–25 [one unnumbered page] 26–178 [179–181].
[i]: title page. [ii]: dedication. [iii–vii]: foreword. [viii]: preface. 1–178:
text; half tone plates facing pages 2, 33, 45, 73, 79, 103, 113, 135, 145,
163, 167. [179–180]: glossary. [181]: blank. Reproduced from typewriting by the Xerox Copyflo process.

Binding: A perfect binding glued in a dark purplish-blue (201) smooth
buckram lettered across the front cover in gold: 'ADVENTURES|WITH|
THE IRISH BRIGADE'. Edges trimmed.

Paper: White wove unwatermarked paper.

Contents: Foreword. pp. [iii–vii].

Notes: By Mr C. C. Gunner, a school friend of Larkin's, the book
deals with his wartime experiences; it was written in 1973 and privately
produced for Mr Gunner in an edition of twenty-four copies delivered
to the author on 14 August 1975.

B18   SHAKESPEARE-PREIS   1976

STIFTUNG F.V.S. ZU HAMBURG|Verleihung des|SHAKESPEARE-
PREISES 1976|an|Philip A. Larkin|C.B.E., M.A., D.Lit., D.Litt.,
F.R.S.L.|Hull|am 20. April 1976

Collation: 8¹⁄₁₂×5⅝ in. [205×145 mm.] [1]²[2–4]⁸, pp. [1–2] 3–7 [8]
9–24 [25–26] 27–37 [38] 39–45 [46–51] 52.
[1]: title page. [2]: obverse of the presentation medal. 3–4: history of
the prize. 5–7: Burgomaster's welcome. [8]: blank. 9–16: citation of
Larkin. 17–24: German translation of Larkin's reply. [25]–45: English
version of the preceding; 26 and 38 blank. [46]: blank. [47–51]:
appendix giving the text of the award; 50 blank. 52: photographic
credits.

Binding: Stapled four times and glued in a white card cover lettered

across the front cover in black: 'STIFTUNG F.V.S. ZU HAMBURG |
[ornament: a fountain] | SHAKESPEARE-PREIS | 1976'; and on the rear
cover: '[ornament: a fortress tower on a heath] | Printed in Germany'.

Paper: White shiny loaded paper.

Contents: Address by Philip Larkin. pp. 39–45.
        German translation on pp. 17–24.

Notes: Distributed by the Foundation in December 1976 in an edition
of 1,200 copies at no charge.

C

CONTRIBUTIONS BY
PHILIP LARKIN
TO
PERIODICALS

1933

C1   Getting up in the morning. *The Coventrian*, 143 (December 1933), 965.

1936

C2   Reflections at Christmastide. *The Coventrian*, 152 (December 1936), 270.

1937

C3   A quiet snooze. *The Coventrian*, 153 (March 1937), 326.

C4   A garden is a lovesome thing . . . *The Coventrian*, 154 (July 1937), 349–51.

C5   Parting is such sweet sorrow. *The Coventrian*, 155 (December 1937), 393–4.

1938

C6   Fears of the brave. *The Coventrian*, 156 (April 1938), 449–51.

C7   Winter nocturne: Mantled in grey, the dusk steals slowly in . . . Fragment from May: Stands the Spring!—heralded by its bright-clothed . . . *The Coventrian*, 158 (December 1938), 559–60.

C8   "Thou was not born for death, immortal bird . . . " *The Coventrian*, 158 (December 1938), 560–1.

1939

C9   Summer nocturne: Now night perfumes lie upon the air . . . *The Coventrian*, 159 (April 1939), 593.

C10   Cleanliness is next to . . . ? *The Coventrian*, 159 (April 1939), 596–7.

C11   We protest [editorial by H. E. A. Roe and P. A. Larkin]. *The Coventrian*, 159 (April 1939), 586–7.

C12   Letter to the Editor [signed by] P. A. Larkin [and] F. G. Smith. *The Coventrian*, 159 (April 1939), 609.

C13   Happy fields. *The Coventrian*, 160 (September 1939), 640–2.

C14   Street lamps: When night slinks, like a puma, down the sky . . . *The Coventrian*, 160 (September 1939), 644.

C15   K.H.S. in Brussels, Easter 1939 [by H. E. A. Roe and P. A. Larkin]. *The Coventrian*, 160 (September 1939), 631–3.

C16   Fifty years back [by H. E. A. Roe and P. A. Larkin]. *The Coventrian*, 160 (September 1939), 633–5.

1940

C17 Spring warning: And the walker sees the sunlit battlefield . . .
The Coventrian, 161 (April 1940), 689.

C18 Last will and testament: Anxious to publicise and pay our
dues . . . [by B. N. Hughes and P. A. Larkin]. *The Coventrian*,
162 (September 1940), 734–5.
Dated 26 July 1940.

C19 Ultimatum: But we must build our walls, for what we are . . .
Listener, XXIV, 620 (28 November 1940), 776.

1941

C20 Story: Tired of a landscape known too well when young . . .
Cherwell, LXI, 4 (13 February 1941), 50.

C21 A writer: "Interesting, but futile", said his diary . . . *Cherwell*,
LXII, 2 (8 May 1941), 20.
Listed on the cover of the issue dated 2 May 1941 but not then
included.

C22 May weather: A month ago in fields . . . *Cherwell*, LXII, 6
(5 June 1941), 92.

C23 Conscript: The ego's county he inherited . . . *Phoenix* (Ayton),
III, 1 (October–November 1941), 14.

C24 Observation: Only in books the flat and final happens . . .
O[xford] U[niversity] L[abour] C[lub] *Bulletin*, III, 7 ([22
November 1941]), 10.

1942

C25 Disintegration: Time running beneath the pillow wakes . . .
O[xford] U[niversity] L[abour] C[lub] *Bulletin*, ([February
1941]), [Not seen].

C26 Sonnet: This was your place of birth, this daytime palace . . .
Cherwell, LXIII, 7 (28 February 1942), 76. Signed "R.L." in
error.

1943

C27 Mythological introduction: A white girl lay on the grass . . .
Poem: I dreamed of an out-thrust arm of land . . . *Arabesque*,
[2] (Hilary term 1943), 5.

1946

C28 Plymouth: A box of teak, a box of sandalwood . . . Portrait:
Her hands intend no harm . . . *Mandrake*, 3 (May 1946), 19.

1949

C29   Reading habits [letter]. *Library Association Record*, LI, 11 (November 1949), 358–9.

1950

C30   Distant prospects, by Charles Russell [*i.e.* P. A. Larkin]. *Luciad* (University College, Leicester), n.s.1 (January 1950), 6–8.

1952

C31   Bertrand Russell and D. H. Lawrence [letter]. *Radio Times* [Northern Ireland edition only], CXVI, 1497 (18 July 1952), 4.

C32   Review [of] *Afternoon Men*, by A. Powell. Q (Queen's University, Belfast), 7 (Michaelmas 1952), 35–6.

1953

C33   Psychology and vivisection [letter]. *New Statesman*, XLV, 1156 (2 May 1953), 519.

C34   Wires: The widest prairies have electric fences . . . *Spectator*, CXCI, 6536 (2 October 1953), 367.

C35   Hand and Flower press [letter]. *Listener*, L, 1285 (15 October 1953), 647.

1954

C36   Fiction and the reading public: Give me a thrill, says the reader . . . *Essays in Criticism*, IV, 1 (January 1954), 86.
       Written in 1950.

C37   Triple time: This empty street, this sky to blandness scoured . . . *Poetry and Audience*, 8 (28 January 1954), 8.

C38   Latest face: Latest face, so effortless . . . *Spectator*, CXCII, 6558 (5 March 1954), 258.
       Written in February 1951.

C39   Triple time: This empty street, this sky to blandness scoured . . . *Spectator*, CXCII, 6566 (30 April 1954), 513.

C40   Not literary enough. *Poetry and Audience*, 21 (10 June 1954), [1]-3.
       A review of *A Charm against the Toothache*, by J. Heath-Stubbs.

C41   Poetry of departures: Sometimes you hear, fifth-hand . . . *Poetry and Audience*, 21 (10 June 1954), 6.

C42   Toads: Why should I let the toad work . . . *Listen*, I, 2 (Summer 1954), 15–16.

C43   Age: My age fallen away like white swaddling . . . Skin: Obedient daily dress . . . *Spectator*, CXCIII, 6575 (2 July 1954), 15.

C44   Born yesterday: Tightly folded bud . . . *Spectator*, CXCIII, 6579 (30 July 1954), 144.
        Dedicated to Sally Amis.

C45   Myxomatosis: Caught in the centre of a soundless field . . . *Spectator*, CXCIII, 6596 (26 November 1954), 682.

C46   Poetry of departures: Sometimes you hear, fifth-hand . . . *Listen*, I, 3 (Winter 1954), 2.

1955

C47   Times, places, loved ones: No, I have never found . . . *Spectator*, CXCIV, 6602 (7 January 1955), 18.

C48   Always too eager for the future, we . . . *Departure*, III, 7 (Spring 1955), 4-5.

C49   If, my darling: If my darling were once to decide . . . *Shenandoah*, VI, 2 (Spring 1955), 31.

C50   Since we agreed to let the road between us . . . *Departure*, III, (Summer 1955), 12.

C51   Mr Bleaney: 'This was Mr Bleaney's room. He stayed . . . The importance of elsewhere: Lonely in Ireland, since it was not home . . . *Listener*, LIV, 1384 (8 September 1955), 373.

C52   I remember, I remember: Coming up England by a different line . . . *Platform*, 4 (Autumn 1955), 24.

C53   Arrivals, departures: This town has docks where channel boats come sidling . . . Line on a young lady's photograph album: At last you yielded up the album, which . . . Q (Queen's University, Belfast), 11 (Hilary [Autumn] 1955), 29-30.

C54   Beyond a joke. Q (Queen's University, Belfast), 11 (Hilary [Autumn] 1955), 39-43.
        A review of *A few late Chrysanthemums*, by J. Betjeman.

C55   Referred back: *That was a pretty one*, I heard you call . . . *Listen*, I, 4 (Autumn 1955), 8.

C56   Church going: Once I am sure there's nothing going on . . . *Spectator*, CXCV, 6647 (18 November 1955), 665.

1956

C57   Abstract vision. *Manchester Guardian*, 17 April 1956, p. 4.
        A review of *Collected Poems*, by K. Raine.

C58 An Arundel tomb: Side by side, their faces blurred . . . *London Magazine*, III, 5 (May 1956), 33–4.

C59 [Letter.] *London Magazine*, III, 6 (June 1956), 72.

C60 No more fever. *Listen*, II, 1 (Summer 1956), 22–6. A review of *The Shield of Achilles*, by W. H. Auden.

C61 Ignorance: Strange to know nothing, never to be sure . . . *Listen*, II, 1 (Summer 1956), 4.

C62 Waiting for breakfast: Waiting for breakfast while she brushed her hair . . . *Poetry Book Society Bulletin*, 10 (July 1956), [1].

C63 Shem the penman. *Manchester Guardian*, 3 July 1956, p. 4. A review of *Dublin's Joyce*, by H. Kenner.

C64 At first: Lambs that learn to walk in snow . . . *Times Educational Supplement*, 46th year, 2147 (13 July 1956), 933.

C65 The importance of elsewhere: Lonely in Ireland, since it was not home . . . *Humberside* (Hull Literary Club), XII, 2 (Autumn 1956), 31.
"Reprinted by kind permission of the Editor of *The Listener*".

C66 Chosen and recommended. *Manchester Guardian*, 16 October 1956, p. 4.
A review of *Green with Beasts*, by W. S. Merwin and *Poems from the North*, by K. Nott.

C67 For Sydney [*sic*] Bechet: That note you hold, narrowing and rising, shakes . . . *Ark*, 18 (November 1956), 58.

C68 Mr Bleaney: "This was Mr. Bleaney's room. He stayed . . . *New World Writing*, 10th Mentor selection (November 1956), 148.

C69 An Arundel tomb: Side by side, their faces blurred . . . *Poetry and Audience*, IV, 6 (16 November 1956), 2–3.

C69a Separate ways. *Manchester Guardian*, 30 November 1956, p. 14. A review of *A Case of Samples*, by K. Amis.

1957

C70 Pigeons: On shallow slates the pigeons shift together . . . *Departure*, IV, 11 (January 1957), 2.

C71 You do something first. *Manchester Guardian*, 29 January 1957, p. 4.
A review of *Stanzas in Meditation and Other Poems, 1920–1933*, by G. Stein and *Gertrude Stein: her Life and Work*, by E. Sprigge.

C72 Success story: *To fail* (transitive and intransitive) . . . *The*

Grapevine (University of Durham Institute of Education), 4 (February 1957), 8.

C73   Miss Ridler and Miss Millay. *Manchester Guardian*, 26 March 1957, p. 4.
A review of *The trial of Thomas Cranmer*, by A. Ridler, *Collected Poems* of Edna St. Vincent Millay, and *Section rockdrill 85–95 de los cantores*, by E. Pound.

C74   Tops: Tops heel and yaw . . . *Listen*, III, 2 (Spring 1957), 6.

C75   An Arundel tomb: Side by side, their faces blurred . . . *Torch* (University of Hull), VII, 4 (Easter 1957), 25–6.

C76   The mighty Mezz. *Truth*, CLVII, 4205 (26 April 1957), 477–8.
A review of *Really the blues*, by M. Mezzrow and B. Wolfe.

C77   The writer in his age: Philip Larkin. *London Magazine*, IV, 5 (May 1957), 46–7.

C78   Poetry at present. *Manchester Guardian*, 7 May 1957, p. 4. A review of *The Romantic Survival*, by J. Bayley and *Poetry in our Time*, by B. Deutsch.

C79   Recent verse—some near misses. *Manchester Guardian*, 4 June 1957, p. 4.
A review of *The Minute and Longer Poems*, by J. Holloway; *Union Street*, by C. Causley, *Poems, 1943–1956*, by R. Wilbur, and *Visitations*, by L. MacNeice.

C80   Ideas about poetry. *Manchester Guardian*, 23 July 1957, p. 4.
A review of *Romantic Image*, by F. Kermode, and *The Poetry of Experience*, by R. Langbaum.

C81   The new Bohemia. *Truth*, CLVII, 4218 (26 July 1957), 861.
A review of *Jazzmen*, ed. by F. Ramsey, Jr., and C. E. Smith; *Eddie Condon's Treasury of Jazz*, ed. by E. Condon and R. Gehman; and *Count Basie and his Orchestra*, by R. Horrocks.

C82   Days: What are days for? . . . Water: If I were called in . . . *Listen*, II, 3 (Summer–Autumn 1957), [1].

C83   The pleasure principle. *Listen*, II, 3 (Summer–Autumn 1957), 28–32.
A review of *A Mortal Pitch*, by V. Scannell; *Devil, maggot and son*, by C. Logue; and *Uncertainties and Other Poems*, by J. Press.

C84   Jazz. *Truth*, CLVII, 4237 (6 December 1957), 1395. A review of *The story of jazz*, by M. Stearns.

C85   Success story: *To fail* (transitive and intransitive) . . . *Beloit Poetry Journal*, VIII, 2 (Winter 1957–58), 36.

1958

C86 [A review of] *Thomas Hardy and the Cosmic Mind* . . . by J. O. Bailey. *Modern Language Review*, LIII, 1 (January 1958), 116.

C87 The importance of elsewhere: Lonely in Ireland, since it was not home . . . *Listen*, II, 4 (Spring 1958), 2.

C88 Referred back: *That was a pretty one*, I heard you call . . . *Paris Review*, 19 (Summer 1958), 37.

C89 Two poems. Days: What are days for . . . Water: If I were called in . . . *Poetry and Drama Magazine*, X, 2 (1958), 24. Reprinted from *Listen* Summer–Autumn 1957.

C90 Harsh and bitter-sweet. *Manchester Guardian*, 13 June 1958, p. 4. A review of *King Joe Oliver*, by W. C. Allen and B. A. L. Rust, and *Lady sings the blues*, by B. Holiday.

C91 Bad bold beauty. *Manchester Guardian*, 29 August 1958, p. 4. A review of *A History of Jazz in America*, by B. Ulanov; *A Handbook of Jazz*, by B. Ulanov; and *The Decca Book of Jazz*, ed. by P. Gammond.

C92 Reports on experience. *Manchester Guardian*, 5 September 1958, p. 6. A review of *A Sense of the World*, by E. Jennings; *To Whom it may Concern*, by A. Ross; and *Poetry for Supper*, by R. S. Thomas.

C93 Such sweet thunder. *Manchester Guardian*, 30 September 1958, p. 4. A review of *Duke Ellington*, ed. by P. Gammond, and *Second Chorus*, by H. Lyttelton.

C94 Modesties: Words plain as hen-birds' wings . . . *Humberside* (Hull Literary club), XIII, 1 (Autumn 1958), 29.

C95 Authors' manuscripts [letter]. *Times Literary Supplement*, 57th year, 1954 (10 October 1958), 577.

C96 Mouldie figges. *Manchester Guardian*, 7 November 1958, p. 6. A review of *The heart of Jazz*, by W. L. Grossman and J. W. Farrell.

C97 No fun any more. *Manchester Guardian*, 18 November 1958, p. 4. A review of *The Chequer'd Shade*, by J. Press.

C98 Graves superior. *Manchester Guardian*, 2 December 1958, p. 4. A review of *Steps*, by R. Graves. See also the subsequent statement printed in the issue for 30 December 1958, p. 3.

C99   Poetry beyond a joke. *Manchester Guardian*, 19 December 1958, p. 4.
      A review of *Collected Poems*, by J. Betjeman.

1959

C100 West Britons and true Gaels. *Manchester Guardian*, 20 February 1959, p. 5.
      A review of *The Oxford Book of Irish Verse*, ed. by D. Mac-Donagh and L. Robinson.

C101 Blues from the brickyards. *Manchester Guardian*, 20 March 1959, p. 10.
      A review of *The Book of Jazz*, ed. by L. Feather and other titles.

C102 [A review of] *The Industrial Muse*, ed. by J. Warburg. *Modern Language Review*, LIV, 2 (April 1959), 300.

C103 Betjeman en bloc. *Listen*, III, 2 (Spring 1959), 14–22.
      A review of *Collected Poems*, by J. Betjeman.

C104 Not the place's fault. *Umbrella*, I, 3 (Spring 1959), [107]–12.

C105 Some jazz books. *Torch* (University of Hull), May 1959, pp. 22–5.

C106 Keeping up with the Graveses. *Manchester Guardian*, 15 May 1959, p. 6.
      A review of *Collected Poems*, by R. Graves; *Life Studies*, by R. Lowell; *Homage to Mistress Bradstreet*, by J. Berryman; *Songs*, by C. Logue; and *Poems*, by R. Taylor.

C107 Jazz in society. *Observer*, 31 May 1959, p. 25.
      A review of *The Jazz Scene*, by F. Newton.

C108 Look, no kangaroos. *Australian Letters*, II, 1 (June 1959), 31–3.
      A review of *Act One*, by R. Stow, and *Antipodes in Shoes*, by G. Dutton.

C109 The Whitsun weddings: That Whitsun I was late getting away . . . *Encounter*, XII, 6 (June 1959), 47–8.

C110 Four early poems. I. I see a girl dragged by the wrists . . . II. The bottle is drunk out one by one . . . III. Like the train's beat . . . Song. 65° N. My sleep is made cold . . . *Poetry Northwest*, I, 1 (June 1959), 8–11.

C111 Music of the negro. *Manchester Guardian*, 31 July 1959, p. 5.
      A review of *The Jazz Scene*, by F. Newton, and *These Jazzmen of our Time*, by R. Horrocks.

C112   The savage seventh. *Spectator*, CCIII, 6856 (20 November 1959), 713–14.
A review of *The Lore and Language of Schoolchildren*, by I. and P. Opie.

C113   Texts and symbols. *Guardian*, 27 November 1959, p. 11.
A review of *Cypress and Acacia*, by V. Watkins, and *A Matter of Life and Death*, by A. Ridler.

C114   [A review of] *Guy Fawkes Night and Other Poems*, by J. Press. *Critical Quarterly*, I, 4 (Winter 1959), 362–3.

C115   Down among the dead men. *Spectator*, CCIII, 6860 (18 December 1959), 912.
A review of *Georgian Poets*, selected by A. Pryce-Jones; *Collected Poems* of Sir John Squire; and *The Skylark and Other Poems*, by R. Hodgson.

1960

C116   Imaginary museum piece. *Guardian*, 1 January 1960, p. 6.
A review of *The Forests of Lithuania*, by D. Davie, and *One and One*, by P. J. Kavanagh.

C117   Hounded. *Spectator*, CCIV, 6867 (5 February 1960), 188.
A review of *Francis Thompson*, by J. C. Reid.

C118   Lice, fleas and gullible mayflies. *Guardian*, 5 February 1960, p. 6.
A review of *The Masks of Love*, by V. Scannell, and *The Collector and Other Poems*, by P. Redgrove.

C119   Collected poems. *Guardian*, 25 March 1960, p. 9.
A review of *Collected Poems*, vol. 3 by R. Campbell.

C120   A racial art. *Observer*, 27 March 1960, p. 21.
A review of *Blues fell this Morning*, by P. Oliver.

C121   Before tea: Summer is fading . . . *Listen*, III, 3–4 (Spring 1960), 5.

C122   A real musicianer. *Guardian*, 8 April 1960, p. 15.
A review of *Treat it gentle*, by S. Bechet, and *This is Jazz*, ed. by K. Williamson.

C123   Carnival in Venice. *Spectator*, CCIV, 6879 (29 April 1960), 630.
A review of *The Holy Barbarians*, by L. Lipton.

C124   Gleanings from a poor year for poetry. *Guardian*, 29 April 1960, p. 10.
A review of *The Guinness Book of Poetry, 1958–59*; *Collected poems*, by E. Muir; and *The Gravel Ponds*, by P. Levi.

In relation to this review see also the note by Larkin in the *Guardian*, 17 May 1960, p. 8.

C125   Library fines [letter]. *Torchlight* (University of Hull), 35 (10 May 1960), 2.

C126   Exhumation. *Spectator*, CCIV, 6882 (20 May 1960), 742.
A review of *The Buried Day*, by C. Day Lewis.

C127   The University of Hull's new library. *Library Association record*, LXII, 6 (June 1960), 185–9.

C128   Last-but-one round-up. *Guardian*, 10 June 1960, p. 8.
A review of *Collected Poems*, by W. Plomer.

C129   What's become of Wystan? *Spectator*, CCV, 6880 (15 July 1960), 104–5.
A review of *Homage to Clio*, by W. H. Auden.

C130   Faith healing: Slowly the women file to where he stands . . . *Listener*, LXIV, 1634 (21 July 1960), 115.
Broadcast on 24 July 1960 in the Third Programme.

C131   MCMXIV: Those long uneven lines . . . *Saturday Book*, 20 ([10 October] 1960), 153–4.

C132   The critic as hipster. *Guardian*, 25 November 1960, p. 10. A review of *The Sound of Surprise*, by W. Balliett, and *Jazz*, ed. by N. Hentoff and A. MacCarthy.

C133   A study of reading habits: When getting my nose in a book . . . *Critical Quarterly*, II, 4 (Winter 1960), 351.

C134   Talking in bed: Talking in bed ought to be easiest . . . *Texas Quarterly*, III, 4 (Winter 1960), 193.

C135   The blending of Betjeman. *Spectator*, CCV, 6910 (2 December 1960), 913.
A review of *Summoned by Bells*, by J. Betjeman.

1961

C136   Echoes of the Gatsby era. *Daily Telegraph*, 11 February 1961, p. 11.

C137   As good as a mile: Watching the shied core . . . *Audit* (University of Buffalo), I, 2 (28 March 1960), 2.

C138   Benny's immortal hour. *Daily Telegraph*, 11 March 1961, p. 11.
On Benny Goodman.

C139   Ambulances: Closed like confessionals, they thread . . . *London Magazine*, I, 1 n.s. (April 1961), [23].

C140   The growth of the blues. *Daily Telegraph*, 15 April 1961, p. 11.

C141 Bands across the sea. *Daily Telegraph*, 13 May 1961, p. 11.
C142 Better than the best. *Daily Telegraph*, 10 June 1961, p. 6. On Sidney Bechet and Charlie Parker.
C143 Naturally the Foundation will bear your expenses: Hurrying to catch my Comet . . . *Twentieth Century*, CLXX, 1010 (July 1961), 54.
C144 The large cool store: The large cool store selling cheap clothes . . . *Times Literary Supplement*, 60th year, 3098 (14 July 1961), supp. i.
C145 Folk heroes in bowlers. *Daily Telegraph*, 15 July 1961, p. 9.
C146 Putting the moderns in their place. *Daily Telegraph*, 12 August 1961, p. 9.
      A review of *The real Jazz*, by H. Panassié (revised edition).
C147 Post-holiday recuperation. *Daily Telegraph*, 9 September 1961, p. 9.
C148 With not-so-silent friends. *Guardian*, 15 September 1961, p. 7.
      A review of *Essays on Jazz*, by B. James.
C149 Missing chairs. *New Statesman*, LXII, 1594 (29 September 1961), 440.
      A review of *Collected Verse from 1929 on*, by O. Nash.
C150 MCMXIV: Those long uneven lines . . . *Poetry Review*, LII, 4 (October–December 1961), 201.
C151 Survival of the hottest. *Daily Telegraph*, 14 October 1961, p. 11.
      On Charles "Pee Wee" Russell.
C152 Breadfruit: Boys dream of native girls who bring breadfruit . . . *Critical Quarterly*, III, 4 (Winter 1961), 309.
C153 Trumpet preliminary. *Daily Telegraph*, 11 November 1961, p. 11.
      On Louis Armstrong.
C154 Lives of the poets. *Guardian*, 24 November 1961, p. 12.
      A review of *Django Reinhardt*, by C. Delaunay.
C155 Here: Swerving east, from rich industrial shadows . . . *New Statesman*, LXII, 1602 (24 November 1961), 788.
C156 Ambulances: Closed like confessionals, they thread . . . *Atlantic*, CCVIII, 6 (December 1961), 62.
C157 Bunk's boy. *Guardian*, 1 December 1961, p. 9.
      A review of *Call him George*, by J. Allison.
C158 Horn of a dilemma. *Daily Telegraph*, 9 December 1961, p. 11.
      On Bix Beiderbecke.

C159   Critics' choice: Philip Larkin. *Guardian*, 15 December 1961, p. 9.

C160   Jazz records of the year. *Daily Telegraph*, 18 December 1961, p. 10.

1962

C161   Faith healing: Slowly the women file to where he stands . . . *Shenandoah*, XIII, 2 (Winter [*i.e.* January] 1962), 33.

C162   The spell of Basin street. *Daily Telegraph*, 13 January 1962, p. 9.

C163   Poetic heritage, 328. Wants: Beyond all this, the wish to be alone . . . *Sunday Times*, 21 January 1962, p. 11.
Reprinted from TLD.

C164   Broadcast: Giant whispering and coughing from . . . *Listener*, LXVII, 1713 (25 January 1962), 157.

C165   Nothing to be said: For nations vague as weed . . . *London Magazine*, I, 11 n.s. (February 1962), 5-6.

C166   Poetry 1962: context [Philip Larkin, 31-2]. *London Magazine*, I, 11 n.s. (February 1962), 27-54.

C167   Masters' voices. *New Statesman*, LXIII, 1612 (2 February 1962), 170-1.
A review of *Poetry and the Physical Voice*, by F. Berry; *A Sequence for Francis Parkman*, by D. Davie; and other poetry recordings.

C168   Ellington minus the Duke. *Daily Telegraph*, 10 February 1962, p. 11.

C169   American poetry [letter]. *Times Literary Supplement*, 61st year, 3131 (2 March 1962), 137.

C170   Young revolutionaries. *Daily Telegraph*, 10 March 1962, p. 11.

C171   Mrs Hardy's memories. *Critical Quarterly*, IV, 1 (Spring 1962), 75-9.
A review of *Some Recollections*, by E. Hardy, ed. by E. Hardy and R. Gittings.

C172   Old hands in new sleeves. *Daily Telegraph*, 16 April 1962, p. 15.

C172a   [Obituary for Miss Agnes] Cuming. *Library Association record*, LXIV, 5 (May 1962), 194.

C173   Contrasting equals. *Daily Telegraph*, 14 May 1962, p. 17.
On Charlie Parker and Louis Armstrong.

C174   [A review of] *The Story of the Original Dixieland Jazz Band*, by H. O. Brunn. *Listener*, LXVII, 1731 (31 May 1962), 962, 964.

C175   Voices from the south. *Daily Telegraph*, 16 June 1962, p. 11.

C176   Grace notes from outer space. *Daily Telegraph*, 14 July 1962, p. 9.
       On Ornette Coleman.

C177   Fact and fiction. *Daily Telegraph*, 11 August 1962, p. 9. A review of *Strike the Father dead*, by J. Wain and other titles.

C178   The poetry of William Barnes. *Listener*, LXVIII, 1742 (16 August 1962), 257.
       A review of *The Poems of William Barnes*, ed. by B. Jones.

C179   Big noise from yesterday. *Daily Telegraph*, 8 September 1962, p. 9.

C180   For Sydney [*sic*] Bechet: That note you hold, narrowing and rising, shakes . . . *Listen*, IV, 1 (Autumn 1962), 8.

C181   Should jazz be an art? *Observer*, 8934, 23 September 1962, p. 29
       A review of *The Reluctant Art*, by B. Green.

C182   Frivolous and vulnerable. *New Statesman*, LXIV, 1646 (28 September 1962), 416, 418.
       Reprinted on the sleeve of *Stevie Smith reads and comments on selected poems* (Listen LPV 7 [1966]).

C183   Essential beauty: In frames as large as rooms that face all ways . . . *Spectator*, CCIX, 7006 (5 October 1962), 530.

C184   Holiday in spring and summer. *Daily Telegraph*, 17 October 1962, p. 12.
       On Billie Holiday.

C185   Larkin talks on jazz [report of an introductory talk and record recital to the English Society]. *Torchlight* (University of Hull), 69 (23 October 1962), 6.

C186   Essential beauty: In frames as large as rooms that face all ways . . . *The Balkite* (Perry Jackson Grammar School Magazine, Doncaster), Special Issue (November 1962), [25].
       Reprinted, with an appreciation by M. Wagstaff, from C183.

C187   Open your Betjemans. *Spectator*, CCIX, 7011 (9 November 1962), 726.
       A review of *A Ring of Bells*, by J. Betjeman.

C188   Jam yesterday. *Daily Telegraph*, 10 November 1962, p. 11.
       On the Commodore Music Shop and its records.

C189   Send no money: Standing under the fobbed . . . *Observer*, 8942, 18 November 1962, p. 24.

C190   Toads revisited: Walking around in the park . . . *Spectator*, CCIX, 7013 (23 November 1962), 828.

C191   Real cool alley. *Daily Telegraph*, 15 December 1962, p. 9.

C192   Records of the year: jazz. *Daily Telegraph*, 17 December 1962, p. 10.

1963

C193   Tender voices. *Torch* (University of Hull), (1963), [2–3].

C194   Sunny Prestatyn: *Come to Sunny Prestatyn* . . . *London Magazine*, II, 10 n.s. (January 1963), 13.

C195   The prospect behind us. *Daily Telegraph*, 12 January 1963.

C196   Wild oats: About twenty years ago . . . *The Review*, 5 (February 1963), 11.

C197   Dominant come-lately. *Daily Telegraph*, 9 February 1963, p. 11.

C198   Groupings. *Spectator*, CCX, 7025 (15 February 1963), 202.
       A review of *The Powys brothers*, by R. C. Churchill, and *Ronald Firbank and John Betjeman*, by J. Brooke.

C199   Ambassadors extraordinary. *Daily Telegraph*, 20 March 1963, p. 11.
       On Benny Goodman.

C200   [A review of] *Jazz and the White American*, by N. Leonard. *Tempo*, 64 (Spring 1963), 37–8.

C201   Freshly scrubbed potato. *Guardian*, 5 April 1963, p. 13.
       A review of *The Complete Poems* of W. H. Davies, and *W. H. Davies: a critical biography*, by R. Stonesifer.

C202   Dockery and Son: 'Dockery was junior to you . . . *Listener*, LXIX, 1776 (11 April 1963), 633.

C203   Legend of the jungle. *Daily Telegraph*, 17 April 1963, p. 10.
       On James "Bubber" Miley.

C204   Pianists not for shooting. *Daily Telegraph*, 15 May 1963, p. 12.
       On Thomas "Fats" Waller.

C205   The death of the blues? *Daily Telegraph*, 12 June 1963, p. 10.

C206   Pieces of string. *Daily Telegraph*, 10 July 1963, p. 10.
       On Joe Venuti and Eddie Lang.

C207   Battle without conflict. *Daily Telegraph*, 10 August 1963, p. 11.

C208   On the wing. *Guardian*, 6 September 1963, p. 8.
       A review of *Bird: the Legend of Charlie Parker*, by R. H. Reisner.

C209   Louis MacNeice. *New Statesman*, LXVI, 1695 (6 September 1963), 294.

C210   A cool look at Bird. *Daily Telegraph*, 11 September 1963, p. 12.
       On Charlie Parker.

C211   The thundering herds of Woody Herman. *Daily Telegraph*, 9 October 1963, p. 12.

C212 The war poet. *Listener*, LXX, 1802 (10 October 1963), 561–2. A review of *The Collected Poems* of Wilfred Owen, ed. by C. Day Lewis.

C213 Miles without end. *Daily Telegraph*, 30 October 1963, p. 10. On Miles Davis.

C214 Atmospheric pressure. *Daily Telegraph*, 13 November 1963, p. 12.

C215 Take one home for the kiddies: On shallow straw, in shadeless glass . . . *Listener*, LXX, 1810 (5 December 1963), 955.

C216 As bad as a mile: Watching the shied core . . . *Listener*, LXX, 1811 (12 December 1963), 985.

C217 As it was in the old days. *Daily Telegraph*, 14 December 1963, p. 11.

C218 Records of the year: jazz. *Daily Telegraph*, 23 December 1963, p. 9.

1964

C219 My best record of 1964. *Daily Telegraph*, 11 January 1964, p. 11.

C220 Home is so sad: Home is so sad. It stays as it was left . . . *Listener*, LXXI, 1817 (23 January 1964), 149.

C221 Philip Larkin writes . . . ; Modesties: Words as plain as hen-birds' wings . . . *Poetry Book Society Bulletin*, 40 (February 1964), 1–2.

C222 Out of the hustle. *Daily Telegraph*, 8 February 1964, p. 11.

C223 Modesties: Words as plain as hen-birds' wings . . . *Encounter*, XXII, 3 (March 1964), 28.

C224 Mafeking relieved. *Daily Telegraph*, 4 March 1964, p. 12.

C225 Monk in the daylight. *Daily Telegraph*, 25 March 1964, p. 14. On Thelonius Monk.

C226 [A review of] *Christina Rossetti*, by L. M. Packer [and] *The Rossetti-Macmillan letters*, ed. by L. M. Packer. *Listener*, LXXI, 1826 (26 March 1964), 526.

C227 New Orleans preserv'd. *Daily Telegraph*, 15 April 1964, p. 14.

C228 Declining night music. *Daily Telegraph*, 13 May 1964, p. 14.

C229 Naturally the Foundation will bear your expenses: Hurrying to catch my Comet . . . *Partisan Review*, XXXI, 3 (Summer 1964), [381].

C230 When rocker goes mod. *Daily Telegraph*, 10 June 1964, p. 14. On Charles "Pee Wee" Russell.

C231 Timbres varied. *Spectator*, CCXIII, 7098 (10 July 1964), 54–5.

A review of *Dinosaurs in the Morning*, by W. Balliett, and *Swing Photo Album 1939*, by T. Rosencrantz.

C232   Shakespeare, thou art translated. *Daily Telegraph*, 18 July 1964, p. 11.
On John Dankworth and Cleo Laine.

C233   Grouse shoot [letter]. *Daily Telegraph*, 13 August 1964, p. 14.

C234   Mingus=Duke Minus. *Daily Telegraph*, 15 August 1964, p. 11.
On Charlie Mingus.

C235   From clubs to concerts. *Daily Telegraph*, 9 September 1964, p. 12.
On the magazine *Downbeat*.

C236   Odyssey for old-timers. *Daily Telegraph*, 7 October 1964, p. 14.

C237   Shouting v. moaning. *Daily Telegraph*, 4 November 1964, p. 12.

C238   The incomparable Max. *Daily Telegraph*, 27 November 1964, p. 17.
A review of *My Life in Jazz*, by M. Kaminsky; *The Josh White Song Book*, and *The Penguin Book of American Folk Songs*, by A. Lomax.

C239   Memories of festivals past. *Daily Telegraph*, 9 December 1964, p. 14.

C240   Records of the year: jazz. *Daily Telegraph*, 21 December 1964, p. 13.

1965

C241   Toads revisited: Walking around in the park . . . *New York Review of Books*, III, 11 (14 January 1965), 11.
Reprinted from TWW.

C242   Unnatural breaks. *Daily Telegraph*, 16 January 1965, p. 15.

C243   Baffling sax and baroque piano. *Daily Telegraph*, 15 February 1965, p. 17.
On Sonny Rollins.

C244   Melody Maker jazz poll special: Philip Larkin. *Melody Maker*, 20 February 1965, p. ii.

C245   A little night music. *Daily Telegraph*, 17 March 1965, p. 14.
On Don Byas.

C246   Giving the bird to the legend. *Daily Telegraph*, 7 April 1965, p. 14.
On Charlie Parker.

C247   Requiem for jazz. *Weekend Telegraph* [colour supplement to the *Daily Telegraph*], 23 April 1965, pp. [27 and 29–30].

C248 Testifyin' to the blues tradition. *Guardian*, 30 April 1965, p. 8.
A review of *Conversation with the Blues*, by P. Oliver, and *Music on My Mind*, by W. Smith.

C249 So fast is so high. *Daily Telegraph*, 5 May 1965, p. 16.
On Bud Powell.

C250 Prelusive poems. *Torch* (University of Hull), ([June] 1965), [17]–18.
A review of *Twelve Poems* by N. Jackson.

C251 Alive from New Orleans. *Daily Telegraph*, 9 June 1965, p. 14.
On Sidney Bechet.

C252 Way out in all directions. *Daily Telegraph*, 12 July 1965, p. 15.
On John Coltrane.

C253 Dixieland rolled into one. *Daily Telegraph*, 9 August 1965, p. 15.

C254 The price of an anthology [letter]. *Times Literary Supplement*, 64th year, 3313 (26 August 1965), 735.

C255 Twenties swan song. *Daily Telegraph*, 15 September 1965, p. 14.

C256 Straight and true. *Daily Telegraph*, 13 October 1965, p. 14.
On Billie Holiday.

C257 Lovely gigs. *Guardian*, 29 October 1965, p. 8.
A review of *Owning-up*, by G. Melly.

C258 Davis declaimed. *Daily Telegraph*, 10 November 1965, p. 14.
On Miles Davis.

C259 The Django life. *Daily Telegraph*, 8 December 1965, p. 14.
On Django Reinhardt and others.

C260 Records of the year: jazz. *Daily Telegraph*, 20 December 1965, p. 13.

1966

C261 Cults and criticism. *Daily Telegraph*, 9 February 1966, p. 14.

C262 Correction [letter on the date of Bix Beiderbecke's death]. *Torchlight* (University of Hull), 107 (17 February 1966), 4.

C263 Bessie Smith alone. *Daily Telegraph*, 9 March 1966, p. 14.

C264 The new wave smoothed out. *Daily Telegraph*, 6 April 1966, p. 15.

C265 Young contemporaries. *Torch* (University of Hull), (May 1966), 23, 25.

C266 The end of a swinging era. *Daily Telegraph*, 4 May 1966, p. 14.
A review of *Jazz Records A–Z, 1932–1942*, by B. Rust.

C267 Didn't they ramble. *Guardian*, 20 May 1966, p. 7.

A review of *Fourteen Miles on a Clear Night*, by P. Gammond and P. Clayton.

C268   Solar: Suspended lion face . . . *Queen*, CCCCXXVI, 5594 (25 May 1966), 47.

C269   Love: The difficult part of love . . . *Critical Quarterly*, VIII, 2 (Summer 1966), 173.

C270   Wanted: good Hardy critic. *Critical Quarterly*, VIII, 2 (Summer 1966), 174–9.
A review of *Thomas Hardy: the Will and the Way*, by R. Morrell.

C271   Fats Waller and his formula. *Daily Telegraph*, 1 June 1966, p. 12.

C272   Very good friend. *Guardian*, 8 July 1966, p. 12.
A review of *Ain't Misbehavin'*, by E. Kirkeby.

C273   Bond's last case. *Spectator*, CCXVII, 7202 (8 July 1966), 50, 52.
A review of *Octopussy* and *The Living Daylights*, by I. Fleming.

C274   Flute between two waves. *Daily Telegraph*, 11 July 1966, p. 10.
On Eric Dolphy.

C275   Ambulances: Closed like confessionals, they thread . . . *Observer* [colour magazine], 14 August 1966, p. 12.

C276   Basie at his best. *Daily Telegraph*, 21 September 1966, p. 12.

C277   Soul food. *Guardian*, 7 October 1966, p. 13.
A review of *Urban blues*, by C. Keil.

C278   Lloyd does something pretty. *Daily Telegraph*, 19 October 1966, p. 14.
On Charles Lloyd.

C279   Guitarist to Goodman. *Daily Telegraph*, 16 November 1966, p. 12.
On Charlie Christian.

C280   Foreword. *Poet's Eye* [Hull], 1 ([December 1966]), [3].

C281   Bop-master Brown. *Daily Telegraph*, 5 December 1966, p. 9.
On Clifford Brown.

C282   Records of the year: jazz. *Daily Telegraph*, 19 December 1966, p. 13.

1967

C283   Friday night in the Royal Station hotel: Light spreads darkly downwards from the high . . . *Morning Telegraph* [Sheffield], 7 January 1967, p. 12.

C284   Gulliver's travails. *Guardian*, 13 January 1967, p. 7.
A review of *Shadow and Act*, by R. Ellison.

C285   Purist of a sort. *Daily Telegraph*, 20 February 1967, p. 9.

C286 Ducal mystique. *Daily Telegraph*, 15 March 1967, p. 14.
On Duke Ellington.

C287 Funny old hat. *Daily Telegraph*, 12 April 1967, p. 14.

C288 The confidence of Coleman. *Daily Telegraph*, 10 May 1967, p. 14.
On Ornette Coleman.

C289 Not as wild as his name. *Daily Telegraph*, 7 June 1967, p. 14.
On "Wild Bill" Davison.

C290 Disagreeable to unbearable. *Guardian*, 7 July 1967, p. 5.
A review of *The Jazz Cataclysm*, by B. McRae.

C291 In the front seat. *Daily Telegraph*, 10 July 1967, p. 8.
On Luis Russell.

C292 Jazzmen. *Spectator*, CCXIX, 7259 (11 August 1967), 163–4.
A review of *Four Lives in the Bebop Business*, by A. B. Spellman.

C293 Superlatively alone. *Guardian*, 18 August 1967, p. 5.
A review of *The Life that late he Led*, by G. Eells.

C294 How Rushing went on singing. *Daily Telegraph*, 27 September 1967, p. 12.
On Jimmy Rushing.

C295 In the mainstream manner. *Daily Telegraph*, 18 October 1967, p. 16.

C296 How distant: How distant, the departure of young men . . .
Listener, LXXVIII, 2013 (26 October 1967), 521.

C297 Panassié in New Orleans. *Daily Telegraph*, 8 November 1967, p. 12.
On Hugues Panassié and Milton 'Mezz' Mezzrow.

C298 Sympathy in white major: When I drop four cubes of ice . . .
London Magazine, VII, 9 n.s. (December 1967), 13.

C299 The vintage years. *Daily Telegraph*, 6 December 1967, p. 12.

C300 Records of the year: jazz. *Daily Telegraph*, 18 December 1967, p. 12.

1968

C301 History: Sexual intercourse began . . . *Cover* [Oxford], 1 February 1968, p. 12.
Omits one line in error.

C302 Past and future freedoms. *Daily Telegraph*, 10 February 1968, p. 13.
On Leonard Feather in the magazine *Melody Maker*.

C303   White-hot blues. *Daily Telegraph*, 9 March 1968, p. 13.
       On Louis Armstrong.

C304   Surname unadorned [letter]. *The Times*, 11 March 1968, p. 9.

C305   Surname unadorned [letter]. *The Times*, 28 March 1968, p. 11.

C306   The New Yorker beat. *Guardian*, 29 March 1968, p. 11.
       A review of *Such Sweet Thunder* by W. Balliett.

C307   Blowing British. *Daily Telegraph*, 13 April 1968, p. 13.

C308   Holroyd's Strachey [letter]. *Times Literary Supplement*, 67th year, 3453 (2 May 1968), 457.

C309   Dear old Dixie. *Daily Telegraph*, 11 May 1968, p. 15.
       On the Original Dixieland Jazz Band.

C310   The trees: The trees are coming into leaf . . . *New Statesman*, LXXV, 1940 (17 May 1968), 659.

C311   Nostalgia corner. *Daily Telegraph*, 8 June 1968, p. 15.

C312   The Apollo bit. *New Statesman*, LXXV, 1944 (14 June 1968), 798-9, 802.
       A review of *The Letters of Rupert Brooke*, ed. by Sir G. Keynes.

C313   Two poems. Posterity: Jake Balokowsky, my biographer . . . Sad steps: Groping back to bed after a piss . . . *New Statesman*, LXXV, 1946 (28 June 1968), 876.

C314   Aretha's gospel. *Daily Telegraph*, 13 July 1968, p. 13.
       On Aretha Franklin.

C315   Philip Larkin praises the poetry of Thomas Hardy. *Listener*, LXXX, 2052 (25 July 1968), 111.
       Extracted from a broadcast "A man who noticed things" on BBC Radio 4.

C316   The inimitable Jimmy Yancey. *Daily Telegraph*, 10 August 1968, p. 14.

C317   Poets' manuscripts [letter]. *Times Literary Supplement*, 67th year, 3469 (22 August 1968), 897.

C318   Byways of the blues. *Guardian*, 6 September 1968, p. 7.
       A review of *Screening the Blues*, by P. Oliver.

C319   Twilight of the old gods. *Daily Telegraph*, 14 September 1968, p. 16.
       On Henry "Red" Allen and Charles "Pee Wee" Russell.

C320   In presenting Mr Robert Forrester Drewery to the Chancellor, the Librarian delivered the following oration . . . *University of Hull Gazette*, XI, 1 (Autumn 1968), 14.

C321   Friday night in the Royal Station hotel: Light spreads darkly downwards from the high ... *Humberside* (Hull Literary club), XVI, I (Autumn 1968), 33.

C322   When they still made nice noises. *Daily Telegraph*, 12 October 1968, p. 15.

C323   Laying down light fiction. *Daily Telegraph Magazine*, 8 November 1968, p. 57.
A selection of titles.

C324   Amazing Armstrong. *Daily Telegraph*, 9 November 1968, p. 13.
On Louis Armstrong.

C325   Permissions [letter]. *Times Literary Supplement*, 68th year, 3536 (4 December 1968), 1405.
Signed by Larkin and seven others.

C326   Two sides to Hodges. *Daily Telegraph*, 14 December 1968, p. 13.
On Johnny Hodges.

C327   Records of the year: jazz. *Daily Telegraph*, 16 December 1968, p. 12.

1969

C328   Just a little while. *Daily Telegraph*, 11 January 1969, p. 19.
On George Lewis.

C329   Homage to a government: Next year we are to bring the soldiers home ... *Sunday Times*, 19 January 1969, p. 60.

C330   Curling up with a good record. *Torchlight* (University of Hull), 20 February 1969, p. 8.

C331   Critic among elusive labels. *Daily Telegraph*, 8 February 1969, p. 15.

C332   Poets in a fine frenzy and otherwise. *Guardian*, 13 February 1969, p. 7.
A review of *Poems and Poets*, by G. Grigson.

C333   When blues are taken as read. *Daily Telegraph*, 8 March 1969, p. 15.

C334   The most Victorian laureate. *New Statesman*, LXXVII, 1983 (14 March 1969), 363–4.
A review of *The Poems of Tennyson*, ed. by C. Ricks.

C335   Vernon Watkins: an encounter and a re-encounter. *Mabon*, I, I (Spring 1969), 6–10.

C336   The rummagers. *Daily Telegraph*, 12 April 1969, p. 13.

C337   Record-making history. *Daily Telegraph*, 10 May 1969, p. 15.
On the Commodore Music shop and its records.

C338   A revival that came too late. *Daily Telegraph*, 14 June 1969, p. 15.
On Johnny Dodds.

C339   Armstrong out on his own. *Daily Telegraph*, 12 July 1969, p. 15.
On Louis Armstrong and others.

C340   Unacknowledged legislators. *Guardian*, 31 July 1969, p. 5.
A review of *The Story of the Blues*, by P. Oliver.

C341   Squalor behind the blues. *Daily Telegraph*, 9 August 1969, p. 13.

C342   Music to stand up to. *Guardian*, 4 September 1969, p. 9.
A review of *Black Music*, by L. Jones, and *Tales*, by L. Jones.

C343   Going more chromatic than pop. *Daily Telegraph*, 13 September 1969, p. 13.
On be-bop.

C344   Expectations keep reputations alive. *Daily Telegraph*, 18 October 1969, p. 15.

C345   Swinging ancient and modern. *Daily Telegraph*, 8 November 1969, p. 9.
On Eddie Condon.

C346   Just around the corner. *Daily Telegraph*, 13 December 1969, p. 10.

C347   Records of the year: jazz. *Daily Telegraph*, 22 December 1969, p. 4.

1970

C348   Two poems. To the sea: To step over the low wall that divides . . . Annus mirabilis: Sexual intercourse began . . . *London Magazine*, IX, 10 n.s. (January 1970), 28–9.

C349   Taste of the past. *Daily Telegraph*, 10 January 1970, p. 7.
On the magazine *Downbeat*.

C350   Grub Vale. *Guardian*, 12 February 1970, p. 9.
A review of *Edward Thomas: a Critical Biography*, by W. Cook.

C351   Making the most of the big band. *Daily Telegraph*, 14 February 1970, p. 9.

C352   Off beat [letter]. *Spectator*, CCXXIV, 7393 (7 March 1970), 318.

C353   Big victims: Emily Dickinson and Walter de la Mare. *New Statesman*, LXXIX, 2035 (13 March 1970), 367–8. A review of *The Complete Poems* of Emily Dickinson, and *The Complete Poems* of Walter de la Mare.

C354   Bursting-out of the blues. *Daily Telegraph*, 14 March 1970, p. 9.

C355 Copyright of letters [letter]. *The Times*, 11 April 1970, p. 9.
C356 The colour of their music. *Daily Telegraph*, 18 April 1970, p. 11.
C357 Copyright of letters [letter]. *The Times*, 22 April 1970, p. 11.
C358 Fragments of a golden age. *Daily Telegraph*, 9 May 1970, p. 10. On the big bands of the 1930s.
C359 More toads re-visited [extracts from the citation by Dr P. A. Larkin on the presentation of Cecil Day Lewis for the honorary degree of Doctor of Letters, University of Hull]. *The Review*, 22 (June 1970), 59–60.
C360 Supporting groups make history. *Daily Telegraph*, 20 June 1970, p. 10. On Billy Banks.
C361 Student poetry: Philip Larkin looks at some poems by students from Hull. *Torch* (University of Hull), Summer 1970, pp. 25–7.
C362 Annus mirabilis: Sexual intercourse began . . . *Michigan Quarterly Review*, IX, 3 (Summer 1970), 146.
C363 Looking back at Lyttelton. *Daily Telegraph*, 11 July 1970, p. 8. On Humphrey Lyttelton.
C364 Onwards and downwards. *Daily Telegraph*, 15 August 1970, p. 6. A retort to hostile critics of AWJ.
C365 In presenting Cecil Day-Lewis to the Vice-Chancellor on 2 May 1970, Dr P. A. Larkin delivered the following oration . . . *University of Hull Gazette*, XIII, 1 (Autumn term 1970), 13–14.
C366 How: How high they build hospitals . . . *Wave*, 1 (Autumn 1970), 32.
C367 Listening with a difference. *Daily Telegraph*, 12 September 1970, p. 8.
C368 Two poems. Dublinesque: Down stucco sidestreets . . . The cardplayers: Jan van Hogspeuw staggers to the door . . . *Encounter*, XXXV, 4 (October 1970), 41.
C369 Where Europe is unrivalled. *Daily Telegraph*, 10 October 1970, p. 12. A review of *Who's Who in Jazz*, by J. Chilton.
C370 Trial of faith. *Daily Telegraph*, 21 November 1970, p. 9.
C371 [A review of] *Your Jazz Collection*, by D. Langridge. *Library Association record*, LXXII, 12 (December 1970), 379.
C372 Alive and well. *Daily Telegraph*, 12 December 1970, p. 9. On Duke Ellington and Louis Armstrong.

C373   Records of the year: jazz. *Daily Telegraph*, 21 December 1970, p. 4.

1971

C374   Not much doing, man. *Daily Telegraph*, 25 January 1971, p. 5.

C375   Mr Powell's mural. *New Statesman*, LXXXI, 2083 (19 February 1971), 243–4.
A review of *Books do Furnish a Room*, by A. Powell.

C376   Miss Bessie to you. *Daily Telegraph*, 13 March 1971, p. 11. On Bessie Smith.

C377   The literature of jazz [by D. Kennington; letter relating to a previous review]. *Times Literary Supplement*, 70th year, 3604 (26 March 1971), 353.

C378   Formal opening of the extension of the Brynmor Jones library . . . 16th December 1970 . . . thanking Lord Cohen the Librarian, Dr P. A. Larkin, said . . . *University of Hull Gazette*, XIII, 2 (Spring 1971), 9.

C379   In white tie and tails, *Daily Telegraph*, 16 April 1971, p. 11. On British bands of the 1930s.

C380   Sounds of yesterday. *Daily Telegraph*, 15 May 1971, p. 9. On Ornette Coleman.

C381   Hardy's mind and heart. *Daily Telegraph*, 3 June 1971, p. 7. A review of *Hardy's Vision of Man*, by F. R. Southerington, and *Thomas Hardy: his Career as a Novelist*, by M. Millgate.

C382   Voices as instruments. *Daily Telegraph*, 12 June 1971, p. 10. On the Mills Brothers, Ella Fitzgerald and others.

C383   Vers de société: *My wife and I have asked a crowd of craps* . . . *New Statesman*, LXXXI, 2100 (18 June 1971), 854.

C384   From trad to the other thing. *Daily Telegraph*, 10 July 1971, p. 7.

C385   Cut grass: Cut grass lies frail . . . *Listener*, LXXXVI, 2209 (29 July 1971), 144.

C386   Palgrave's last anthology: A. E. Housman's copy. *Review of English Studies*, n.s. XXII, 87 (August 1971), 312–16.

C387   Armstrong's last good-night. *Daily Telegraph*, 21 August 1971, p. 7.

C388   Jazz-man's sound and fury. *Daily Telegraph*, 26 August 1971, p. 6.
A review of *Beneath the Underdog*, by C. Mingus.

C389   In presenting Norman Higson to the Chancellor, Dr P. A.

Larkin delivered the following oration . . . *University of Hull Gazette*, XIV, 1 (Autumn term 1971), 14–15.

C390 It could only happen in England [John Betjeman]. *Cornhill*, 1069 (Autumn 1971), 21–36.

C391 The trees: The trees are coming into leaf . . . *Humberside* (Hull Literary club), XVII, 1 (Autumn 1971), 11.

C392 Among the ducal portraits. *Daily Telegraph*, 18 September 1971, p. 7.
On Duke Ellington.

C393 Satchmo still. *Guardian*, 21 October 1971, p. 14.
A review of *Louis*, by M. Jones and J. Chilton, and *Louis Armstrong: the Interview*, by R. Meryman.

C394 Wedding-wind: The wind blew all my wedding-day . . . Going: There is an evening coming in . . . Water: If I were called in . . . Days: What are days for? . . . Winter: In the field, two horses . . . At grass: The eye can hardly pick them out . . . Wants: Beyond all this, the wish to be alone . . . *Recognitions* [Dundas, Ontario], 2 (Winter 1971), [2–3].

C395 A question of environment [letter]. *Torchlight*, (University of Hull), 2 December 1971, p. 4.

C396 Sounds of a veterans' rally. *Daily Telegraph*, 11 December 1971, p. 9.
On the World's Greatest Jazz Band.

C397 Books of the year: Philip Larkin. *Observer*, 19 December 1971, p. 17.

1972

C398 Cut off for Christmas [letter]. *The Times*, 6 January 1972, p. 11.

C399 Stevie, good-bye. *Observer*, 23 January 1972, p. 28. A review of *Scorpion and Other Poems*, by S. Smith.

C400 Livings: I deal with farmers, things like dips and feed . . . *Observer*, 20 February 1972, p. 28.

C401 [A review of] *Champion of a Cause*, by A. MacLeish. *Journal of Documentation*, XXVIII, 1 (March 1972), 72–3.

C402 The building: Higher than the handsomest hotel . . . *New Statesman*, LXXXIV, 2139 (17 March 1972), 356.

C403 In Benny Goodman's golden days. *Daily Telegraph*, 20 April 1972, p. 10.

C404 Heads in the women's ward: On pillow after pillow lies . . . *New Humanist*, I, 1 (May 1972), 17.

C405 The hidden Hardy. *New Statesman*, LXXXIII, 2150 (2 June 1972), 752–3.
A review of *One fair woman: Thomas Hardy's letters to Florence Henniker*, 1893–1922, ed. by E. Hardy and F. B. Pinion.

C406 Prologue: I thought it would last my time . . . *Observer*, 4 June 1972, p. 11.

C407 Hull poetry lectureship [letter]. *Times Literary Supplement*, 71st year, 3668 (16 June 1972), 689.

C408 The state of poetry—a symposium: Philip Larkin. *The Review*, 29–30 (Spring–Summer 1972), 60.

C409 Bull fighting [letter]. *The Times*, 13 July 1972, p. 17.

C410 The explosion: On the day of the explosion . . . *Listener*, LXXXVIII, 2264 (17 August 1972), 208.

C411 Lucky old England's poet [John Betjeman]. *Sunday Telegraph*, 15 October 1972, p. 20.

C412 Supreme sophisticate. *Punch*, CCLXIII, 6894 (25 October 1972), 587.
A review of *Cole*, by R.Kimball.

C413 Library licences [letter]. *Library Association record*, LXXIV, 11 (November 1972), 224–5.

C414 Negroes of Europe. *Guardian*, 30 November 1972, p. 21.
A review of *Pop Music and Blues*, by R. Middleton.

C415 The Strachey Trust [letter]. *Times Literary Supplement*, 71st year, 3693 (15 December 1972), 1533.

C416 The old fools: What do they think has happened, the old fools . . . *Listener*, LXXXIX, 2288 (1 February 1973), 147.

C417 'Twentieth century English verse' [letter]. *Times Literary Supplement*, 72nd year, 3708 (30 March 1973), 353.

C418 Larkin's anthology [letter]. *Listener*, LXXXIX, 2297 (5 April 1973), 449.

C419 'A great parade of single poems'—Philip Larkin . . . discusses his 'Oxford book of twentieth century verse' with Anthony Thwaite. *Listener*, LXXXIX, 2298 (12 April 1973), 472–3.

C420 Oxford book [letter]. *Times Literary Supplement*, 72nd year, 3712 (27 April 1973), 473.

C421 Larkin's anthology [letter]. *Listener*, LXXXIX, 2303 (17 May 1973), 654.

C422 Bessie and Billie. *Guardian*, 24 May 1973, p. 11.
A review of *Bessie*, by C. Albertson, and *Lady sings the Blues*, by B. Holiday and W. Dufty.

C423 Birdlife. *Guardian*, 28 June 1973, p. 15.
      A review of *Bird lives*, by R. Russell.

C424 On John Betjeman: a citation. *Encounter*, XLI, 3 (September 1973), 17.
      The citation for the award of an honorary degree at the University of Hull.

C425 Name names [letter]. *Times Higher Education Supplement*, 102 (28 September 1973), 12.

C426 In presenting Sir John Betjeman to the Vice-Chancellor, Dr Larkin delivered the following oration . . . *University of Hull Gazette*, XVI, 1 (Autumn term 1973), 17–19.
      Also issued for the ceremony itself in a 3ff. mimeographed form.

C427 W. H. Auden (1907–1973). *New Statesman*, LXXXVI, 2220 (5 October 1973), 479.

C428 Articulate devotion. *Observer*, 21 October 1973, p. 40.
      A review of *The Faber Book of Love Poems*, ed. by G. Grigson, and *The Penguin Book of Love Poetry*, ed. by J. Stallworthy.

C429 The trees: The trees are coming into leaf . . . To the sea: To step over the low wall that divides . . . *Antaeus*, 12 (Winter 1973), 69–71.

1974

C430 Crit and lit [letter]. *Times Literary Supplement*, 73rd year, 3750 (18 January 1974), 55.

C431 Show Saturday: Grey day for the show, but cars jam the narrow lanes . . . *Encounter*, XLII, 2 (February 1974), [20–1].

C432 Calling the tune. *Daily Telegraph*, 7 February 1974, p. 12.
      A review of *Irving Berlin*, by M. Freedland.

C433 Clear conscience [letter]. *Daily Telegraph*, 13 April 1974, p. 18.
      On bull fighting.

C434 Early days [in the University of Leicester].
      University of Leicester Convocation Review, 1 (August 1974), 10–13.

C435 In the pipeline [letter]. *The Times*, 20 August 1974, p. 13.

C436 That nice boy. *New Statesman*, LXXXVIII, 2275 (25 October 1974), 579, 582.
      A review of *Bix: Man and Legend*, by R. Sudhalter and P. R. Evans with W. Dean-Myatt.

C437 Books of the year. *Observer*, 15 December 1974, p. 19.

1975

C438   Mr Levin's column [letter]. *The Times*, 23 January 1975, p. 17.

C439   The real Wilfred: Owen's life and legends. *Encounter*, XLIV, 3 (March 1975), 73–4, 76–81.
A review of *Wilfred Owen*, by J. Stallworthy.

C440   The Puddletown martyr. *New Statesman*, LXXXIX, 2300 (18 April 1975), 514–15.
A review of *Young Thomas Hardy*, by R. Gittings.

C441   Writers and the closed shop [letter signed by thirteen writers including Larkin]. *Times Literary Supplement*, 74th year, 3817 (2 May 1975), 484.

C442   University photographic service. *University of Hull Bulletin*, 13 (6 June 1975), 2.

C443   Palaeography [notice of a series of lectures]. *University of Hull Bulletin*, 4 (14 November 1975), [1].

C444   Philip Larkin [acceptance speech for the A. C. Benson Silver Medal]. *Reports for 1973–74, list of Fellows and Members for 1975–76*, [December] 1975, p. 47.

C445   P[ublic] L[ending] R[ight]. Philip Larkin. *The New Review*, II, 21 (December 1975), 23–4.

C446   Books of the year: Philip Larkin. *Observer*, 14 December 1975, p. 19.

1976

C447   Opinion. Exams and success, by Britain's prize-winning authors. Philip Larkin. *Sunday Times*, 3 October 1976, p. 15.

C448   Getting the gigs. *Guardian*, 25 November 1976, p. 16.
A review of *All This and 10%*, by J. Godbolt, and *Mahalia*, by A. Goreau.

C449   Books of the year: Philip Larkin. *Observer*, 12 December 1976, p. 26.

D

LARKIN AT THE
UNIVERSITY OF HULL

Larkin was appointed Librarian at the University of Hull on 23 November 1954 and took up his duties on 21 March 1955; since then he has produced many administrative papers and documents for the University, its Senate, the Library Committee and other committees of which he has been or is a member. (For example, he has served as secretary to the Publications Committee since its inception in the session 1957–8.) This bibliography does not set out to record all these documents since they cannot be said to have been published. However a certain number were produced for dissemination within, and occasionally without, the University and it seemed proper that any bibliography should record them briefly. Contributions to periodicals published by the University or its student body are listed in section C, and Larkin's part in the tape/slide guide to the Library and the University's publicity film is recorded in section H.

D1   Library [report]. *The University of Hull first report of Council and and report of Senate for the academic year 1st October 1954 to 30th September 1955 and accounts for the year 1st August 1954 to 31st July 1955,* (1955), 38–41.
      About 75 copies were offprinted for private circulation, mainly to other libraries, with a wrapper title reading: 'THE | UNIVER- SITY OF HULL | [university arms] | LIBRARY | Report for the Session 1954–55'.

D2   Library [report]. *The University of Hull second report of Council and report of Senate for the academic year 1st October 1955 to 30th September 1956 . . .* (1956), 37–40.
      About 75 copies were offprinted for private circulation, mainly to other libraries, with a wrapper title reading as above except for the substitution of the dates '1955–56'.

D3   Library [report]. *The University of Hull third report of Council and report of Senate for the academic year 1st October 1956 to 30th September 1957 . . .* (1957), 41–44.
      About 75 copies were offprinted for private circulation, mainly to other libraries.

D4   Library [report]; Publication Committee [report]. *The University of Hull annual report 1957–58,* (1958), 37–42.
      About 75 copies of the Library report were offprinted for private circulation, mainly to other libraries, with a wrapper title reading: 'THE | UNIVERSITY OF HULL | [university arms] | LIBRARY | Report for the Session 1957–58'.

D5   Librarian's annual report, 1958–59; Publications Committee. *The University of Hull annual report, 1958–59*, (1959), 40–46.

About 75 copies of the Library report were offprinted for private circulation, mainly to other libraries, with a wrapper title reading as above except for the substitution of the dates '1958–59'.

D6   Library [report]; Publications Committee. *The University of Hull annual report, 1959–60*, (1960), 49–56.

About 75 copies of the Library report were offprinted for private circulation, mainly to other libraries, with a wrapper title reading as D4 except for the substitution of the dates '1959–60'.

D7   Library [report]; Publications Committee. *The University of Hull annual report, 1960–61*, (1961), 46–52.

About 75 copies of the Library report were offprinted for private circulation, mainly to other libraries, with a wrapper title reading as D4 except for the substitution of the dates '1960–61'.

D8   'THE UNIVERSITY OF HULL | The Library | HANDBOOK FOR | HEADS OF | DEPARTMENT | 1961'

10 × 8 in. [254 × 203 mm.] Six single leaves, pp. [i–ii, 1–2] 3–7 [one unnumbered page] 8 [9].

[i]: title page. [ii]: blank. [1–9]: text; page 2 and the unnumbered page blank.

Stapled twice. The title page is pale pink and serves as a cover. Probably printed in September or October 1961 in an edition of about 50 copies; reproduced from typewriting.

D9   Library [report]; Publications Committee. *The University of Hull annual report, 1961–62*, (1962), 52–60.

About 75 copies of the Library report were offprinted for private circulation, mainly to other libraries, with a wrapper title reading as D4 except for the substitution of the dates '1961–62'.

D10   Library [report]; Publications. *The University of Hull annual report, 1962–63*, (1963), 68–77.

About 100 copies of the Library report were offprinted for private circulation, mainly to other libraries.

Stapled twice in a light-pink (4) card cover lettered across the front cover in black: 'UNIVERSITY OF HULL | The Library | Report for the Session 1962–63'. The colour of the wrapper, the type face and the colour of the ink on this and subsequent similar wrappers were chosen by Larkin.

DII   Library [report]; Publications. *The University of Hull annual report, 1963–64*, (1964), 72–83.

About 100 copies of the Library report were offprinted for private circulation, mainly to other libraries.

Stapled twice in a bluish-white (189) card cover lettered across the front cover in purple as D10 except for the substitution of the dates '1963–64'.

DI2   'THE UNIVERSITY OF HULL | The Library | THE LIBRARY | AND | THE DEPARTMENTS | 1965'.

10 × 8 in. [254 × 203 mm.] Six single leaves, pp. [1–2] 3–12. [1]: preface of 18 lines signed by Larkin. [2]: blank. 3–12: text.

Ring bound with a black plastic comb with pale purplish-pink (252) card covers; the top cover serving as a title page. An enlarged version of D8; probably printed in September or October 1965 in an edition of about 50 copies. Reproduced from typewriting.

DI3   Library [report]; Publications. *The University of Hull annual report, 1964–65*, (1965), 87–99.

About 100 copies of the Library report were offprinted for private circulation, mainly to other libraries.

Stapled twice in a very light yellowish green (134) card cover lettered across the front cover in green as D10 except for the substitution of the dates '1964–65'.

DI4   Library [report]; Publications. *The University of Hull annual report, 1965–66*, (1966), 75–88.

About 100 copies of the Library report were offprinted for private circulation, mainly to other libraries.

Stapled twice in a light orange-yellow (70) card cover lettered across the front cover in brown as D10 except for the substitution of the dates '1965–66'.

DI5   'THE UNIVERSITY'S | LIBRARY | A short account of its present organisation | for all members of staff and for | departmental representatives | in particular'.

10 × 8 in. [254 × 203 mm.] Seventeen single leaves, pp. [2] 1 [2–4] 5–6 [7–10] 11 [12] 13 [14] 15 [16–18] 19–20 [21–22] 23–26 [27–28] 29–32.

[2]: title page; verso quotation from UGC report 1921 and copyright statement. 1: preface. [2]: blank.

[3]–32: text; the title page and pp. 3–4, 7–8, 17–18, 21–2 and 27–8 are on pink paper.

Ring bound with a black plastic comb with strong purplish-pink (247) card covers lettered across the front cover in black: '[fancy] The | University's | Library'. A revised version of D12; probably printed in September or October 1967 in an edition of between 100 and 150 copies. Reproduced from typewriting.

D16   Library [report]; Publications Committee. *The University of Hull annual report, 1966–67*, (1967), 76–91.

About 100 copies of the Library report were offprinted for private distribution, mainly to other libraries.

Stapled twice in a very light greenish-blue (171) card cover lettered across the front cover in dark blue: 'UNIVERSITY OF HULL | The Brynmor Jones Library | Report for the Session 1966–67'.

D17   The Brynmor Jones library [report]; Publications Committee. *The University of Hull annual report, 1967–68*, (1968), 65–80.

About 100 copies of the Library report were offprinted for private circulation, mainly to other libraries.

Stapled twice in a light-orange (52) card cover and lettered across the front cover in grey as D16 except for the substitution of the dates '1967–68'.

D18   'THE NEW BUILDING | The Brynmor Jones Library | University of Hull | 1969'

8×6½ in. [203×163 mm.] Four rectangular leaves folded once, pp. [2, 1] 2–5 [6–7] 8–13 [14].

[2]: title page; verso blank. [1]: preface signed P. A. Larkin. 2–12: text. 13: notes. [14]: blank.

Stapled twice in a strong purplish pink (247) card cover lettered across the front in black: 'THE BRYNMOR JONES LIBRARY | [title in fancy] The | New | Building | UNIVERSITY OF HULL'. Probably printed in May 1969 in an edition of between 3,000 and 4,000 copies. Reproduced from typewriting.

D19   '[title in fancy] The | University's | Library | A short account of its present organisation | for all members of staff and for | departmental representatives | in particular'

9⅞×7 in. [250×176 mm.] Eighteen single leaves, pp. [2] 1 [2–4] 5–7 [8–12] 13 [14] 15 [16–18] 19–20 [21–22] 23–26 [27–28] 29–33 [34].

[2]: title page; verso quotation from UGC report 1921, edition and copyright statements. 1: preface signed P. A. Larkin. [2]:

blank. [3]–33: text; the title page and pp. 3–4, 9–10, 17–18, 21–2 and 27–8 are on pale greenish-yellow paper.
Ring bound with a black plastic comb with light greenish-yellow (101) card covers lettered across the front cover in black: '[fancy] The|University's|Library'. A revised version of D15; probably printed in September or October 1969 in an edition of about 750 copies. Reproduced from typewriting.

D20 The Brynmor Jones library [report]; Publications Committee. *The University of Hull annual report, 1968–69*, (1969), 72–85.
About 150 copies of the Library report were offprinted for private circulation, mainly to other libraries.
Stapled twice in a pale orange-yellow (73) card cover and lettered across the front cover in pale blue as D16 except for the substitution of the dates '1968–69'.

D21 The Brynmor Jones library [report]; Publications Committee. *The University of Hull annual report, 1969–70*, (1970), 74–91.
About 150 copies of the Library report were offprinted for private circulation, mainly to other libraries.
Stapled twice in a very light bluish-green (162) card cover lettered across the front cover in light brown as D16 except for the substitution of the dates '1969–70'.

D22 'The Brynmor Jones Library|READERS'|GUIDE|for Session 1971/72|University of Hull'
8¼×5¾ in. [210×147 mm.] Seven rectangular leaves folded once, pp. 1–28.
1: foreword by the Librarian. 2–28: text.
Stapled twice in strong yellowish-pink (26) card cover; the front cover serves as a title page. Printed in September 1971 in an edition of 3,000 copies. Reproduced from typewriting.

D23 The Brynmor Jones library [report]; Publications Committee. *The University of Hull annual report, 1970–71*, (1971), 73–92.
About 150 copies of the Library report were offprinted for private circulation, mainly to other libraries.
Stapled twice in a pale-yellow (89) card cover lettered across the front cover in light green as D16 except for the substitution of the dates '1970–71'.

D24 'The Brynmor Jones Library|READERS'|GUIDE|1972|University of Hull'
8⅜×5¾ in. [212×145 mm.] Eight rectangular leaves folded once, pp. 1–32.

1: foreword by the Librarian. 2–32: text.

Stapled twice in a light grey (264) card cover; the front cover serves as a title page. Printed in September 1972 in an edition of 3,000 copies.

Larkin's foreword was included unchanged in the issue for 1973 (printed in September 1973 in an edition of 4,000 copies) and this issue was also used, with the addition of an amendment slip pasted on the front page, for the next academic year 1974–5. The *Readers' Guide* for the session 1975–6 (4,000 copies printed in September 1975) uses this foreword unchanged again, and this issue was reprinted (2,500 copies in September 1976) with the addition of a single sheet of addition and amendments for the session 1976–7.

D25   The Brynmor Jones library [report]; Publications Committee. *The University of Hull annual report, 1971–72*, (1972), 80–100.

About 150 copies of the Library report were offprinted for private circulation, mainly to other libraries.

Stapled twice in a light-grey (264) card cover lettered across the front cover in medium purple as D16 except for the substitution of the dates '1971–72'.

D26   The Brynmor Jones library [report]; Publications Committee. *The University of Hull annual report, 1972–73*, (1973), 87–107.

About 150 copies of the Library report were offprinted for private circulation, mainly to other libraries.

Stapled twice in a yellowish-white (92) card cover lettered across the front cover in dark blue as D16 except for the substitution of the dates '1972–73'.

D27   'THE | UNIVERSITY'S | LIBRARY | A short account of its present organisation | for all members of staff and for | departmental representatives | in particular'

$8\frac{1}{4} \times 5\frac{3}{4}$ in. [210 × 148 mm.] Six rectangular leaves folded once, pp. [1–2] 3 [4] 5–22 [23–24].

[1]: title page. [2]: quotation from UGC report 1921, edition and copyright statements. 3: foreword signed P. A. Larkin. [4]: organisation chart. 5–22: text. [23]: blank. [24]: list of library publications.

Stapled twice in a pale yellow (89) card cover lettered across the front cover in black: 'THE | UNIVERSITY'S | LIBRARY'. A revised version of D19; printed in September 1974 in an edition of 1,000 copies. Reproduced from typewriting.

D28   The Brynmor Jones library [report]; Publication Committee.
      The University of Hull annual report, 1973–74, (1974), 39–44.
      A much abridged version of the full reports; the full Library
      report was published separately by the Library and is described
      next.

D29   'UNIVERSITY OF HULL | The Brynmor Jones Library | Report
      for the Session 1973–74'
      $8\frac{1}{4} \times 5\frac{3}{4}$ in. [210 × 147 mm.] Four rectangular sheets folded once,
      pp. 1–16.
      1–11: text. 12–16: statistics and list of staff.
      Stapled twice in a medium orange-yellow (71) card cover; the
      front cover is lettered in light green and serves as title page.
      Printed in January 1975 in an edition of 150 copies. Reproduced
      from typewriting.

D30   The Brynmor Jones library [report]; Publications Committee.
      The University of Hull annual report, 1974–75, (1975), 32–36.
      About 150 copies of the Library report were offprinted in June
      1976 for private circulation, mainly to other libraries.
      Stapled twice in a medium reddish-purple (241) card cover
      lettered across the front cover in black as D16 except for the
      substitution of the dates '1974–75'.

D31   The Brynmor Jones library [report]; Publications Committee.
      The University of Hull annual report, 1975–76, (1976), 30–34.

E

INTERVIEWS

This list of interviews is almost certainly incomplete; however it includes all those interviews which have been traced, even those which are mainly reported speech. Larkin at one time granted interviews fairly readily and the reports by the interviewers are often the surest way of ascertaining his opinions on various topics at those times.

E1   Four young poets I: [interview with] Philip Larkin. *Times Educational Supplement*, 2147 (13 July 1956), p. 933.
Includes the text of the poem "At first".

E2   Arts and the staff: Philip Larkin. *Torchlight* [University of Hull], VIII, 2 (17 March 1959), 5.

E3   The poet-librarian: Gownsman meets Philip Larkin. *Torchlight* [University of Hull], 43 (21 February 1961), 4.

E4   Speaking of writing XIII: [interview with] Philip Larkin. *The Times*, 20 February 1964, p. 16.

E5   Hamilton, Ian. Four conversations. *London Magazine*, n.s. IV, 8 (November 1964), 64–85. [Larkin on pp. 71–7.]

E6   Library clamps down. Mr Larkin speaks of "stricter era". *Torchlight* [University of Hull], 98 (9 March 1965), [1].

E7   Horder, John. A poet on the 8.15. *Guardian*, 20 May 1965, p. 9.

E8   Oakes, Philip. The unsung Gold Medallist. *Sunday Times* [colour magazine], 27 March 1966, pp. 63 and 65.

E9   Poets talking to Mary Holland. *Queen*, CCCCXXVI, 5594 (25 May 1966), 46–7.

E10   A conversation with Philip Larkin. *Tracks*, 1 (Summer 1967), 5–10.

E11   Edmands, Robert. Swinging, swingeing Larkin. *Torchlight* [University of Hull], 6 March 1970, p. 12. Mainly on AWJ.

E12   Philip Larkin talks to *Eboracum*. *Eboracum* [Derwent College, University of York], 10 ([Christmas 1971]), pp. 9 and 16.

E13   Hill, Frances. A sharp-edged view. *Times Educational Supplement*, 2974 (19 May 1972), 19.

E14   Not like Larkin. *Listener*, LXXXVIII, 2264 (17 August 1972), 209. Quoted from the "Larkin at 50" broadcast on BBC Radio 3 on 9 August 1972.

E15   Oliver, Douglas. Profile: poet who captures the music of daily life. *Coventry Evening Telegraph*, 6 October 1972, p. 30.

E16   Gardner, Raymond. Dr Larkin's approach to life and poetry. *Guardian*, 31 March 1973, p. 12.

E17   Binyon, Michael. Public access an "unfair burden" says librarian.
      Times Higher Education Supplement, 27 October 1972, p. 7.
E18   *Green Ginger* interviews major poet Philip Larkin.
      Green Ginger [University of Hull], Spring 1974, pp. 3–4.
E19   Jacobson, Dan. Philip Larkin—a profile. *The New Review*, I,
      3 (June 1974), 25–9.
E20   *The Beverlonian* interview [Steuart Hamilton interviews Philip
      Larkin]. *The Beverlonian* [Beverley Grammar School], XIX, 75
      ([February 1976]), 10–14.

F

RECORDINGS

The section attempts to list and briefly describe first the published and second the unpublished recordings in which Larkin reads his own poems. Each entry for the first section gives a brief transcription of the record title, a physical description of the record itself, a list of the contents and, where possible, some details of the circumstances of the recording and its publication. Entries in the second section are derived principally from BBC Sound Archives and the BBC states that "There is no public access to the Sound Archives section of the BBC and recordings are not normally available except to broadcasters".

PUBLISHED RECORDINGS

FI *Listen presents Philip Larkin reading The Less Deceived.* Listen LPV 1. Hessle, The Marvell Press, [1959].
One 12 in. 33⅓ r.p.m. disc. Matrix: PX 2000 A/B.
Contents: All the poems in the printed volume.
Notes: Recorded 24 October 1958 and released in spring 1959. There is a cancel label reading 'LISTEN' on the disc itself, and another on the reverse of the sleeve reading 'THE MARVELL PRESS | HESSLE, YORKSHIRE'. There is also a signed limited edition of 100 copies with a statement on the reverse of the sleeve reading 'This is No. [number in ink] of a signed limited edition of 100 copies [Larkin's signature in ink]'. (This statement is covered by the cancel label in the ordinary issue.) The limited edition has no cancel label on the actual disc and no matrix number printed on the disc's centre label. The sleeve note outlining the publication history of the book is by Larkin, although unsigned. The front sleeve carries a photograph of Larkin in a cemetery with a bicycle; the rear sleeve has a facsimile of part of the manuscript of "Church Going". The disc was reissued in 1968 with a newly designed sleeve carrying on the front a photograph of Larkin in a cemetery by a monument and on the rear sleeve a transcript of a purported interview with Larkin, actually written by the poet himself. Early in 1976 this recording was issued in cassette form by The Marvell Press. There is a review of the disc by K. Miller in *Spectator*, CCIV (4 March 1960), 330.

F2 *The Jupiter Anthology of Twentieth Century English Poetry*, part III . . . readings directed by V. C. Clinton-Baddeley and edited by Edgar A. Vetter. [London, 1963.]

One 12 in. 33⅓ r.p.m. disc. Matrix: 1/420.

Contents: Side 1: "An Arundel tomb"; "Mr Bleaney".

Notes: Released in November 1963 with sleeve notes by A. Thwaite and sleeve design by O. Lancaster. Released in the United States in 1967 as Folkways record FL 9870.

F3   *Philip Larkin reads and comments on The Whitsun Weddings.* LPV 6. Listen records; the Poets Voice series, edited by George Hartley. Hessle, The Marvell Press, [*c.* 1965].

One 12 in. 33⅓ r.p.m. disc. Matrix: MAR-LP-117 A/B-2U/3U.

Contents: All the poems in the printed volume, with introductory remarks.

Notes: Recorded 20 and 27 September 1964 in the library at the University of Hull and released in October 1965. The front sleeve carries a photograph of Larkin looking out of a train window; the rear sleeve reprints a review of TWW by Christopher Ricks from the *New York Review of Books*, 14 January 1965. Early in 1976 this recording was issued in cassette form by The Marvell Press. There is a review of the disc by David Holloway in the *Daily Telegraph*, 1 December 1965.

F4   *The Poet Speaks*, record 8. Recorded in association with the British Council and the Poetry Room in the Lamont Library of Harvard University. Edited by Peter Orr. Argo PLP 1088. [London], 1967.

One 12 in. 33⅓ r.p.m. disc. Matrix: ARG-2843/4-1/2B.

Contents: Side 1: "Wants"; "Coming"; "Nothing to be said"; "Days"; "Dockery and Son".

Notes: Recorded 27 June 1966 at the University of Hull and released in May 1967. Sleeve design by David Jones; the rear sleeve carries a brief biographical note for Larkin.

F5   *Martin Bell, Muriel Berry, Tony Curtis, Douglas Dunn, Philip Larkin on record.* Yorkshire Arts Association's second recorded anthology of poets reading from their own work; [presented by] Michael Dawson. Yorkshire Arts Association YA3. [Bradford, 1974.]

One 12 in. 33⅓ r.p.m. disc. Matrix: MA YA-3-A/B-1.

Contents: Side 2: "Here"; "Days"; "Next, please"; "Wedding-wind"; "The Whitsun weddings"; "XXX"; "XIII". (Both the last two poems from NS.)

Notes: Recorded 4 February 1974 at the University of Hull and released in October 1974. The rear sleeve carries a brief biographical note for Larkin and included with the disc is a single sheet folded twice printing the texts of all the poems read.

F6　*British poets of our time. Philip Larkin; High windows: poems read by the author.* Edited by Peter Orr. Recorded in association with the Arts Council of Great Britain and the British Council; recording directed by Peter Orr. Argo PLP 1202. [London, *c.* 1975.]

One 12 in. 33⅓ r.p.m. disc. Matrix: ARG-4233/4-IG.

Contents: All the poems in the printed volume.

Notes: Recorded 2 August 1974 at the University of Hull and released in June 1975. The front sleeve carries a reproduction of Edward Ardizzone's painting "Tradesmen's wives at the Shirland"; the rear sleeve carries an introductory note by Clive James.

UNPUBLISHED RECORDINGS

F7　Reading "Lines on a young lady's photograph album"; "Places, loved ones"; "Coming"; "Next, please"; "Going"; "Wants"; "Maiden name"; "No road"; "Church going"; "Age"; "Toads"; "Triple-time"; "Poetry of departures"; "Deceptions"; "I remember, I remember"; "Absences"; "If, my darling"; "Skin"; "Arrivals, departures"; "At grass"; "Mr Bleaney"; "Reference back"; "An Arundel tomb". Recorded by the British Council, 25 March 1958, at Albion House in London. (Tape 295.) Held by the Recorded Sound Section and available for loan.

F8　Interviewed by Ronald Hambledon. "Anthology", Canadian Broadcasting Corporation, ? 1961. Recorded 25 January 1961; Larkin possesses a copy of the recording.

F9　Interviewed on his work and his poetry. "New comment", BBC Third Programme. Recorded 21 June 1961 and broadcast 12 July 1961. (Sound Archives T/29443.)

F10　Interviewed by A. Thwaite; reading "Mr Bleaney". "The world of books", BBC Home Service. Recorded 12 January 1964 and broadcast 29 February 1964. (Sound Archives YLO 33625 from TLO 58855.)

F11　Selecting, introducing and reading his own poems. "The living poet", BBC Third Programme. Recorded 3 July 1964 and broadcast 16 December 1964. (Sound Archives T/29466. TLO 46018.)

FI2 Philip Larkin talks to Peter Orr. Recorded by the British Council at the University of Hull on 27 June 1966. (Tape 1160.) An interview to accompany the recordings of Larkin reading his verse subsequently published in F4. Held by the Recorded Sound Section and available for loan.

FI3 Interviewed by Robert Fox. Radio Australia, ? 1968. Recorded 1 July 1968; Larkin possesses a copy of the recording.

FI4 An appreciation of the poetry of Thomas Hardy. "A man who noticed things", BBC Radio 4 (South and West). Recorded in Leeds by Vernon Scannell on 16 May 1968; broadcast 7 July 1968. (Sound Archives LP 31718.)

FI5 Reading "The Whitsun weddings" and "Home is so sad". "It was always snowing at Christmas", BBC Radio 4. Recorded 6 December 1971 and broadcast 24 December 1971. (Sound Archives T34339.)

FI6 Participating in "Larkin at 50", BBC Radio 3. Recorded 19 June 1972 and broadcast on 9 August 1972. (Sound Archives T36465.) A copy of this recording is held by the British Institute of Recorded Sound (P 832 R).

FI7 Interviewed by Anthony Thwaite on the publication of the *Oxford Book of Twentieth-Century English Verse*, BBC Radio 3. Recorded in March 1973 at the University of Hull and broadcast on 29 March 1973. (Sound Archives MT 36466.) A copy of this recording is held by the British Institute of Recorded Sound (2240 R).

G

RADIO AND TELEVISION APPEARANCES

This list has been compiled on the basis of information from Larkin and from the BBC. It does not attempt to list all the radio and television readings of his poems. For items marked with an asterisk the BBC possess both a script and a recording; for items marked with a dagger a script survived in 1974; and for items marked with a cross a recording alone remained at that date.

G1   Drama. "The arts in Ulster", BBC Northern Ireland, 3 April 1953.

G2   Literature. "The arts in Ulster", BBC Northern Ireland, 7 May 1953.

G3   [Reading "If, my darling".] "First reading", BBC Third Programme, 1 July 1953.

G4   [Reading "Fiction and the reading public".] "New poetry", BBC Third Programme, 8 March 1954.

G5   [Reading "What next; Reasons for attendance".] "New verse", BBC Third Programme, 8 April 1954.

G6   [Introduced by Larkin.] "New poetry", BBC Third Programme, 24 April 1956. Repeated 26 April 1956.

G7   [Reading "An Arundel tomb; Tops; Pigeons".] "Poetry in Hull", BBC North and Northern Ireland, 2 September 1956.

G8   The toneless voice of Robert Graves. BBC Third Programme, 29 June 1959.

G9   [Interviewed by Ronald Hambledon.] "Anthology", Canadian Broadcasting Corporation, ? 1961. Recorded 25 January 1961; not known when the interview was transmitted.

G10*   [Interviewed on his work and his poetry.] "New comment", BBC Third Programme, 12 July 1961. Repeated 23 December 1961.

G11*   [Interviewed by A. Thwaite; reading "Mr Bleaney".] "The World of Books", BBC Home Service, 29 February 1964.

G12†   [Participating in a programme on his poetry and reading "Poetry of departures".] "Poetry today", BBC Third Programme, 1 October 1964.

G13†   [Talking to Sir John Betjeman.] "Monitor", BBC TV1, 15 December 1964. An extract from the film was repeated on BBC TV1 "Tonight", 4 May 1965. One sentence from Larkin is quoted in *Radio Times*, CLXV, 2144 (10 December 1964), 39; a review of the programme by Anthony Burgess is in *Listener*,

LXXIII (3 January 1965), 31. Sometimes titled "Down cemetery road".

G14*   [Selecting, introducing and reading his own poetry.] "The
living poet", BBC Third Programme, 16 December 1964.
Repeated BBC Third Programme, 3 June 1965, and BBC Radio
Three Study Session "Poetry Today, No. 1", 19 July 1965.

G15   [Interviewed on the award of the Queen's Gold Medal for
poetry.] "Today", BBC Home Service, 6 May 1965.

G16   [Reading "Mr Bleaney".] "Read on from here", BBC Home
Service, 7 December 1965. Repeated 6 January 1966.

G17†   [Participating in a programme on Sir] John Betjeman. "The
Masters", BBC Home Service, 25 August 1966.

G18†   [Reading "Church going; Days; At grass".] "Woman's Hour",
BBC Radio 2, 14 November 1967.

G19+   A man who noticed things [Thomas Hardy]. BBC Radio 4
(South and West), 7 June 1968.

G20   [Interviewed by Robert Fox.] Radio Australia, ? 1968. Recorded
1 July 1968; not known when the interview was transmitted.

G21   Louis Armstrong. "The World Tonight", BBC Radio 4,
6 April 1971. (Larkin is doubtful whether this was transmitted
on the date given in the BBC records.)

G22+   [Reading "The Whitsun weddings; Home is so sad".] "It was
always snowing at Christmas", BBC Radio 4, 24 December
1971.

G23*   [Participating in] Larkin at 50: a birthday tribute. BBC Radio
3, 9 August 1972. Repeated on 8 November 1972.

G24*   [Interviewed by A. Thwaite on the publication of *The Oxford
Book of Twentieth-Century Verse*.] BBC Radio 3, 29 March 1973.

G25   [Interviewed by J. Howden on the publication of *High
Windows*.] "Kaleidoscope", BBC Radio 4, 4 June 1974.

G26   [Interviewed by R. Plomley.] "Desert Island Discs", BBC
Radio 4, 17 July 1976. Repeated 19 July 1976.

G27   [Reading and discussing his poetry.] Open University, BBC Radio
4, VHF only, 4 September 1976. Repeated 5 September 1976.

G28   [Interviewed by G. Martin.] Open University, BBC Radio 4,
VHF only, 2 October 1976. Repeated 3 October 1976.

G29   [Participating in] "The Enthusiast" [Sir John Betjeman], BBC
TV2, 22 December 1976. A sentence from Larkin is quoted in
Radio Times, CCXIII, 2771/2 (18 December 1976–1 January
1977), 43, in the notice for this programme.

H

ODDS AND ENDS

This particular section is devoted to a listing of slight or out-of-the-way contributions by Larkin to miscellaneous publications and to recording other works with which he may be said to have had a connection. It has not been possible to include everything which should perhaps have been noted here; for example, the *Shropshire Star* in its issue dated 1 January 1965 asserts, quite incorrectly, that Larkin helped Kingsley Amis with suggestions for the film treatment of "Only Two can Play", the screen version of Amis's novel *That Uncertain Feeling*, which deals with the life of a public librarian, neither have I listed the use of Larkin's poem "Here" in Alan Plater's television play "The Surprise of a Large Town" written in 1967 or 1968 for ABC TV but never produced; Mervyn Morris's poem "Literary evening in Jamaica" in the *Times Literary Supplement*, 9 April 1964, p. 294 (and reprinted in *Caribbean Voices* . . . selected by John Figueroa, vol. 2 (London, Evans, 1970), pp. 181–82); the use of Larkin's poetry in the entertainment "Larkinland" devised by Michael Kustow for the National Theatre and produced there in October and November 1976; Gavin Ewart's gently satirical poem "The Larkin Automatic Car-wash" in his *Be My Guest!* (London, Trigram Press, 1975); Brian Higgins's "Poet to Poet" in *The Northern Fiddler* (London, Methuen, 1966); and various other books dedicated to Larkin (*e.g. Lucky Jim*, by Kingsley Amis; *The Contenders*, by John Wain; and *Courage of Genius*, by Robert Conquest).

H1   *Report of the Public Librarian* ([dated] January 1944), 4pp.; *Annual report*, 1st April 1944–31st March 1945 ([dated] April 1945), 3pp.; *Annual report*, 1st April 1945–31st March 1946 ([dated] May 1946), 3pp.; *Report of the Public Librarian*, January–February 1944 ([dated] 8 March 1944), 2pp.; *Report of the Public Librarian*, March–April 1944 ([dated] 10 May 1944), 2pp.; *Report of the Public Librarian*, May–June 1944 ([dated] 12 July 1944), 2pp.; *Report of the Public Librarian*, July–August 1944 ([dated] 14 September 1944), 2pp.; *Report of the Public Librarian*, September–October 1944 ([dated] 15 November 1944, 2pp.; *Report of the Public Librarian*, November–December 1944 ([dated] 10 January 1945), 3pp.; *Report of the Public Librarian*, January–February 1945 ([dated] 14 March 1945), 2pp.; *Report of the Public Librarian*, March–April 1945 ([dated] 10 May 1945), 2pp.; *Report of Public Librarian*, May–June 1945 ([dated] 19 July 1945), 2pp.; *Report of Librarian*, July–August 1945 ([dated] 11 September 1945), 1p.; *Report of Librarian*, September–October 1945 ([dated] 13 November 1945), 3pp.; *Report of*

Librarian, November–December 1945 ([dated] 8 January 1946,] 2pp.; *Report of Chief Librarian*, January–February 1946 ([dated] 12 March 1946), 2pp.; *Report of Chief Librarian*, March–April 1946 ([dated] 15 May 1946), 2pp.; *Report of Chief Librarian*, May–June 1946 ([dated] 10 July 1946), 2pp.

These mimeographed reports, typed on his own typewriter, were produced by Larkin for his Library Committee while he held the post of Librarian in Wellington. Copies survive in the Wellington Branch of the Salop County Library.

H2 Crispin, Edmund [*i.e.* Bruce Montgomery]. *Holy Disorders*. London Gollancz, 1946.

[p. 6] "Note. My sincere thanks are due to Mr Philip Larkin for reading this book in manuscript and making a number of valuable suggestions. E.C."

H3 Goff, Martyn. *The Flint Inheritance*. London, Andre Deutsch, 1964.

Quotes "Wants" in full on p. 260.

H4 Rowland, J. R. Variations on a theme of Philip Larkin [poem]. *Meanjin Quarterly*, XXIV, 3 (no. 102) (Spring 1965), 287.

H5 *Stevie Smith reads and comments on selected poems*. Listen LPV 7. Hessle, The Marvell press, 1966. Sleeve note by Larkin reprinted from *New Statesman*, 28 September 1962.

H6 *The Brynmor Jones Library*. [A tape/slide guide with commentary spoken by Larkin.] Hull, the University Library, summer 1968. "Since then, the original version has been revised many times. I should think that almost every session there have been revisions of some sort . . . but in 1969 the original presentation was completely outdated by our move into the west extension . . . The presentation shown in October 1970, when we reoccupied the original building . . . must have been a complete revision. By 1972 Philip was dissatisfied with the 1970 version and revised it substantially . . . This revised version was shown in October 1972 and the tape of this performance is the earliest tape we have in the Library . . . The next year it was revised again, and that, the 1973 version, is the current one and also available in the Library" (Brenda Moon, the Deputy Librarian, University of Hull, in a letter to Bloomfield, 23 January 1976.)

H7 *Black paper two: the crisis in education*, ed. by C. B. Cox and A. E. Dyson. [London, Critical Quarterly Society, 1969.]

Two lines quoted on p. 133 "When the Russian tanks roll

westward, what defence for you and me? | Colonel Sloman's Essex Rifles? The Light Horse of L.S.E.?".

H8 Boyle, Harris. A song cycle on poems of Philip Larkin. [I. Dawn. II. Going. III. Night-music.] performed by Patrice Freed, soprano [and] Jeffrey Eschleman, piano. Unpublished. [1970?] Recording in Larkin's possession.

H9 Dunn, Douglas. A Faber melancholy [poem]. *Antaeus*, 6 (Summer 1972), 72–4.
Dedicated to P.L. and I[an] H[amilton].

H10 Open University. Humanities: a foundation course, A100. *The Language of Poetry*: film A100/09, by Graham Martin. Black and white 16 mm sound film. [1973?]
Contains, as part of the sound track, Larkin reading "Here".

H11 'P. A. Larkin (Philip Larkin) has moved to | [six lines within a border of ornaments]'. $5\frac{1}{2} \times 3\frac{1}{2}$ in., postcard, verso blank. [June 1974.]
Change of address card.

H12 University of St. Andrews. *Laureation Addresses*. Graduation ceremonies, 4th and 5th July, 1974. Citation for Dr Philip Larkin, pp. [10–11].

H13 James, Clive. The north window. *Times Literary Supplement*, 3,777 (26 July 1974), 795.
A verse tribute.

H14 Wakeman, John *ed. World Authors, 1950–1975* . . . New York, H. W. Wilson Co., 1975.
An autobiographical note by Larkin on p. 834.

H15 [Larkin quoted in] How to help casualties of library cuts. *Times Higher Education Supplement*, 244 (25 June 1976), p. 6.

H16 *A study in Hull.* The University publicity film, scripted by Professor R. L. Brett. Hull, Audio-Visual Centre University of Hull, [1976].
Includes shots of Larkin at his desk in his office in the Library, and the soundtrack includes him reading the beginning of the poem "Here".

I

MANUSCRIPTS

Larkin retains all his manuscripts and preliminary drafts, with the major exception noted below, and has no plans for their disposal. It is not his practice to make manuscript fair copies of his poems for presentation.

I1 *Manuscript notebook.* [5 October 1944–10 March 1950] Containing autograph drafts and revisions of about eighty-five poems. Presented to the British Library Department of Manuscripts for the Arts Council Collection of Modern Literary Manuscripts (Add. MS 52,619) and fully described by Jenny Stratford in B15, pp. 19–24. The notebook contains drafts for some poems intended for the book *In the Grip of Light* which Larkin prepared for publication in 1948 but which was never published.

I2 Transcript of an interview with Ian Hamilton, annotated by Larkin. *Catalogue*, No. 115, Alan Hancox, [bookseller], item 41, p. 9.
Present whereabouts unknown.

I3 *Jill.* London, Fortune Press, 1946.
A copy of this edition with excisions and occasional amendments by Larkin was used as printer's copy for the Faber edition published in 1964; it was presented by Larkin to the Bodleian Library on 21 April 1965 (Arch. AA e.86).

J

PUBLISHED LETTERS

Letters written to newspapers and periodicals and designed for publication are listed in section C. This section lists the private letters which have found their way, or partial way, into print. Larkin reacts strongly to the unauthorized publication of his private correspondence (including quotations in booksellers' catalogues) and always tries to prevent this happening or secure adequate redress.

J1 April–November 1942. Brief quotations from four letters to Charles Hamblett. [Catalogue] Mommsen, Sevin Seydi, [bookseller], 1974, item 117, p. 52.

J2 2 October 1942; [January?] 1943. Quotations from two letters to Michael Hamburger in his *A Mug's Game: intermittent memoirs, 1924–1954.* [Cheadle Hulme], Carcanet press, [c. 1973], pp. 78–9.

J3 1955. Brief quotation from a letter to a friend. *Catalogue*, no. 114, Alan Hancox, [bookseller], [n.d.], item 167, p. [24].

J4 [1959–60]; [1964]. Brief quotations from four letters to Timothy Rogers. *Catalogue*, no. 960, Bernard Quaritch Ltd., [bookseller], 1976, item 413, p. 46.

J5 [1967?]. Brief quotations from two letters to Ian Hamilton. *Catalogue*, no. 115 "The Review", Alan Hancox, [bookseller], 1969, items 42 and 43, p. 9.

J6 16 August 1972. Letter to Alan Bold in his *Cambridge Book of English Poetry, 1939–1975.* Cambridge, Cambridge University Press, 1976, p. 210.

J7 [1973?]. One sentence from a letter to Alan Ross. *London Magazine*, n.s. XIII, 5 (January 1974), [5].

K

TRANSLATIONS

This is not an exhaustive list of translations of Larkin's work but merely a record of those which have been encountered during the search through indexes and library catalogues for other items. I shall be grateful for notice of any other translations which exist.

CZECH

K1 *Moderní anglická poezie*, ed. by R. F. Willetts. Praha, Mlada Fronta, 1964.
Contains translations of "Church going", "Deceptions", and "Wants". (pp. 153–7)

DUTCH

K2 Philip Larkin. *De revisor* (Amsterdam), II, 5 (November 1975), 27–8.
Contains translations of "Sad steps", "Coming", and "Dublinesque", by Peter Verstegen, and "Going", by T. van Deel.

GERMAN

K3 *Ein Mädchen in Winter* [übertragung von Ruth Welland-Freeman]. Berlin, Volksverband der Bücherfreunde Wegweiser-Verlag, [1948].

K4 Neue Englische Lyrik . . . Philip Larkin. *Ensemble: internationales Jahrbuch fur Literatur*, 4 (1973), 46–53.
Contains translations of "Here", "Going", "Wants", "Afternoons". English and German texts.

K5 Philip Larkin. Thom Gunn. Ted Hughes. *Gedichte*. Berlin, Verlag Volk und Welt, [1974].
Contains translations of poems VIII, X, XVI, XVII, XXI, XXIII, XXIV, XXV, XXVI, XXVIII, XXXI and Songs 65° N, 70° N, 75° N, and Above 80° N all from NS; "Coming", "Going", "Age", "Spring", "Arrivals, departures", "Love songs in age", "For Sidney Bechet", "The Whitsun weddings", "Self's the man", "Days", "Talking in bed", "A study of reading habits", "First sight", and "Wild oats". German and selected English texts.

K6 Address by Philip Larkin [in reply to his citation for the Shakespeare-Preis 1976]. Stiftung F.V.S. zu Hamburg. *Verleihung des*

Shakespeare-Preises 1976 an Philip Larkin . . . an 20. April 1976.
[1976.]
Contains a German translation of Larkin's acceptance speech on
pp. 11–24. The item is more fully described elsewhere (B18).

HUNGARIAN

K7 *Angol költők antológiája,* a valogatast meg kezdte Szabó Lőrinc,
    szerkesz tette es az előszót irta Vajdá Miklos. [Budapest], Móra
    Ferenc Könyvkiadó, [1960]. [Not seen.]
    Contains translations of "Whatever happened" and "Places,
    loved ones", by Anna Hajnal.

K8 Philip Larkin. *Nagyvilág,* XXI, 2 (February 1976), 163–5.
    Contains translations by Desző Tandori of "The trees", "This
    be the verse", "Sad steps", and "Solar".

ITALIAN

K9 Sanesi, Roberto. *Poesia inglese del dopo guerra.* [Milano], Schwarz,
    [c. 1958].
    Contains translations of "Reasons for attendance", "Myxo-
    matosis", "Spring", "If, my darling". English and Italian texts.
    (pp. 182–9)

K10 *Le nozze di Pentecoste e altre poesie . . .* trad. di Renato Oliva e
    Camillo Pennati . . . [Torino], Giulio Einaudi, 1969. (Collezione
    di poesia 64).
    Contains translations of selected poems from NS, TLD and
    TWW with critical introduction. English and Italian texts.

JAPANESE

K11 *Atarashii shi wo yomu—gendai Igirisu, Amerika no shi,* [by]
    Kaneseki Ikio [and others]. Tōkyō, Kenkyū-sha Shuppan, 1972.
    Contains a translation of "Church going" with biographical and
    critical introduction and commentary. English and Japanese
    texts. (pp. 237–53)

POLISH

K12 Nazwisko panieńskie [tr. by Jerzy S. Sito]. *Twórczość,* rok XVI,
    XII (grudzień 1960), 60–1.
    A translation of "Maiden name".

RUSSIAN

K13 *Robert Graves, Dylan Thomas, Ted Hughes, Philip Larkin; perevod s angliiskogo* [compiled and introduced by V. A. Skorodenko, edited by V. S. Murav'ev]. Moskva, "Progress", 1976. Contains translations, by S. Kunyaev, A. Kushner, I. Ozerova, and M. Aliger, of Poems I, II, VI, VIII, IX, X, XI, XVII, XXI, XXIII, XXIV, XXVIII, XXIX, and XXXI from NS; "Lines on a young lady's photographic album", "Places, loved ones", "Next, please", "Wants", "Maiden name", "Church going", "Deceptions", "Poetry of departures", "I remember, I remember", "Arrivals, departures", "At grass", "Here", "Mister Bleaney", "Faith healing", "For Sidney Bechet", "Love songs in age", "Home is so sad", "The Whitsun weddings", "Take one home for the kiddies", "MCMXIV", "The large cool store", "Dockery and Son", "An Arundel tomb", and "To the sea".

SERBO-CROAT

K14 Odlazak [tr. by Vlada Stojikjković]. *Gradina* (Niš), VII, 3–4 (1972), 64. [Not seen.]
A translation of "Poetry of departures".

K15 Poezija odlazaka; Dublinski prizor [tr. by Antun Soljan]. *Književna smotra* (Zagreb), V, 16 (1973), 90–1.
A translation of "Poetry of departures" and "Dublinesque".

K16 Ulazak u crkvu. *Letopis matice srpske* (Novi Sad), CCXIV, 2–3 (August–September 1974), 243–4.
A translation of "Church going".

SWEDISH

K17 *Sommar blir vinter*, till svenska av Britta Gröndahl. [Stockholm], Lars Hökerbergs bokförlag, [1947].

WELSH

K18 Erthygl a Vernon Watkins: Cyfarfod ac Ailgyfarfod. *Mabon*, I, 1 (Gwanwyn 1969), 24–8.

L

ANTHOLOGIES

This section attempts to list anthologies and other compilations re-printing—often for the first time in book form—poems and other writings by Larkin. Larkin's involvement with these books was usually limited only to the granting of permission to reprint; books to which he contributed directly are listed in section B.

The first publication of a poem or essay in book form is indicated by an asterisk.

L1   *Springtime* [one], ed. by G. S. Fraser and Iain Fletcher. London, Peter Owen, [1953].
     Contains: Wedding wind. Deceptions. Since the majority of me . . . On longer evenings . . . Wants. (pp. 60–3)

L2   *New Poems, 1955*, ed. by Patric Dickinson, J. C. Hall, Erica Marx. London, Michael Joseph, [1955].
     Contains: L11. Reasons for attendance. (p. 95)

L3   *New Lines: an Anthology*, ed. by R. Conquest. London, Mac-millan, 1956.
     Contains: Maiden name. Church going. I remember, I remember. Skin. Latest face. Born yesterday. Triple time. Toads. Lines on a young lady's photograph album. (pp. 19–29)

L4   *New Poems, 1956*, ed. by Stephen Spender, Elizabeth Jennings, Dannie Abse. London, Michael Joseph, [1956].
     Contains: *Reference back. *Mr Bleaney. (pp. 88–9)

L5   *New Poems, 1957*, ed. by Kathleen Nott, C. Day Lewis, Thomas Blackburn. London, Michael Joseph, [1957].
     Contains: *An Arundel tomb. (pp. 84–5)

L6   *Best Poems of 1956: Borestone Mountain Poetry Awards 1957 . . . 9th annual issue.* Stanford, Stanford University press, [1957].
     Contains: An Arundel tomb. (pp. 52–3)

L7   *The* [first] *Guinness Book of Poetry, 1956/57.* London, Putnam, 1958.
     Contains: *At first. (p. 74)

L8   *The* [third] *Guinness Book of Poetry, 1958/59.* London, Putnam, [c. 1960].
     Contains: *The Whitsun weddings. (pp. 77–9)

L9   *Poetry and Audience, 1953–60: an Anthology* . . . selected by A. R. Mortimer. [Leeds, Poetry and Audience, 1960?]
     Contains: Poetry of departures. An Arundel tomb. (pp. 39–41)

L10   *The* [fourth] *Guinness Book of Poetry, 1959/60.* London, Putnam, [c. 1961].
     Contains: *Love songs in age. (p. 84)

L11 *New Poems, 1961; a P.E.N. Anthology of Contemporary Poetry*, ed. by William Plomer, Anthony Thwaite, Hilary Corke. London, Hutchinson, [1961].
Contains: *Faith healing. (p. 63)

L12 *The Penguin Book of Contemporary Verse*, ed. by Kenneth Allott. New rev. edn. Harmondsworth, Penguin, 1962.
Contains: Church going. Lines on a young lady's photograph album. The Whitsun weddings. (pp. 332–41)

L13 *The* [fifth] *Guinness Book of Poetry, 1960/61*. London, Putnam, [c. 1962].
Contains: *Ambulances. (p. 75)

L14 *The New Poetry*, ed. by A. Alvarez. Harmondsworth, Penguin, 1962.
Contains: Wedding wind. Poetry of departures. Toads. If, my darling. Going. Wants. The Whitsun weddings. Mr Bleaney.

L15 *New Poems, 1962: a P.E.N. Anthology of Contemporary Poetry*, ed. by Patricia Beer, Ted Hughes, Vernon Scannell. London, Hutchinson, [1962].
Contains: Ambulances. (pp. 70–1)

L16 *English Poetry Now*, ed. by. C. B Cox and A. E. Dyson. [Hull, Critical Quarterly, 1962.] (Critical Quarterly Poetry Supplement, No. 3)
Contains: An Arundel tomb. Ambulances. (pp. 2–3)

L17 *New Lines—II: an Anthology*, ed. by Robert Conquest. London, Macmillan, 1963.
Contains: For Sidney Bechet. *Send no money. *Water. The Whitsun weddings. *A study of reading habits. Love songs in age. (pp. 17–23)

L18 *Twentieth Century Love Poems*, ed. by C. B. Cox and A. E. Dyson. [Hull, Critical Quarterly, 1963.] (Critical Quarterly Poetry Supplement, No. 4)
Contains: No road. (p. 20)

L19 *New Poetry 1964*, [ed. by C. B. Cox and A. E. Dyson. Hull, Critical Quarterly, 1964.] (Critical Quarterly Poetry Supplement, No. 5)
Contains: Dockery and Son. Toads revisited. (pp. 6–7)

L20 *Poetry 1967*, selected by C. B. Cox and A. E. Dyson. [London, Critical Quarterly Society, 1967.] (Critical Quarterly Poetry Supplement, no. 8)
Contains: MCMXIV. (p. 19)

L21 *Something To Offer: a Selection of Contemporary Prose and Verse,* ed. by Barbara Lloyd Evans. Glasgow, Blackie and Son, [1968]. *Contains:* Toads. I remember, I remember. Going. A study of reading habits. Modesties.

L22 *Four,* selected by C. B. Cox and A. E. Dyson. [London, Critical Quarterly Society, 1968.] (Critical Quarterly Poetry Supplement, No. 9)
Contains: Church going. No road. The Whitsun weddings. Take one home for the kiddies. (pp. 2–7)

L23 *A Standard of Verse,* by John Moat, with nine poems by Baldwin, Baker, Hughes, Larkin, Levi, Middleton, Murphy, Thomas, Tonks. [Newbury, Berkshire], Phoenix Press, 1969.
Contains: Here. (pp. 39–40)

L24 *Sense and Sensibility in Twentieth Century Writing: a Gathering in Memory of William Van O'Connor,* ed. by Brom Weber, with a preface by Harry T. Moore. Carbondale, Southern Illinois University Press, [1970].
Contains: *How distant. (p. 130)

L25 *Forget-me-not Lane: humourous, serious and dramatic reflections,* by Peter Nichols. London, Faber, 1971.
Contains: [An excerpt from the introduction to *All What Jazz.*] (p. [10])

L26 *By the Tide of Humber: thoughts on Hull and the North Bank,* ed. by Christopher Rowe and Ian Clark. Great Yarmouth, Galliard, [c. 1971].
Contains: Here. (p. 6)

L27 *New Poems 1970–71: a P.E.N. Anthology of Contemporary Poetry,* ed. by Alan Brownjohn, Seamus Heaney, Jon Stallworthy. London, Hutchinson, [1971].
Contains: *To the sea. (pp. 52–3)

L28 *Ezra Pound: the Critical Heritage,* ed. by Eric Homberger. London. Routledge & Kegan Paul, 1972.
Contains: *[An excerpt from a review in the *Manchester Guardian,* 26 March 1957.] (pp. 444–5)

L29 *Poetry 1972,* ed. by Damian Grant. [London, Critical Quarterly Society, 1972.]
Contains: *Livings. (pp. 2–4)

L30 *Poetry Dimension 1,* ed. by Jeremy Robson. [London], Robson Books; Sphere Books, 1973.
Contains: The building. (pp. 120–1)

L31 *Poetry Dimension 2*, ed. by Dannie Abse. [London], Robson
Books; Sphere Books, 1974.
Contains: It could only happen in England. (pp. 13–33)

L32 *New Poems 1975: a P.E.N. Anthology of Contemporary Poetry.*
London, Hutchinson, [1975].
Contains: The life with a hole in it. (p. 97)

Appendix

BIBLIOGRAPHY AND
CRITICISM OF
LARKIN'S WORK

This is an attempt to list all substantive criticism of Larkin's work which has appeared to the end of 1976. It must be said that there is not a great deal and much more criticism is contained in the reviews listed in section A. I have not included most of the material issued in various forms by the Open University nor the similar material issued by the Université de Paris III (Sorbonne Nouvelle) for its "Radio Correspondance" which produced a programme on Larkin on 23 October 1973 (repeated 26 November 1973) for the Agrégation examination. This list is divided into four sections: the first lists books devoted to Larkin; the second, books parts of which deal with Larkin; the third, articles in periodicals; and the fourth, theses and academic dissertations.

BOOKS

1. Brownjohn, Alan. *Philip Larkin* . . . ed. by Ian Scott-Kilvert. [London], Longman Group for the British Council, [1975]. (Writers and their work, No. 247)
2. Day, Roger. *Philip Larkin* . . . [Milton Keynes], Open University Press, [1976]. (Arts: A Third Level course. Twentieth century poetry, unit 28. A 306 28)
3. Kuby, Lolette. *An Uncommon Poet for the Common Man: a Study of Philip Larkin's Poetry*. The Hague, Mouton, 1974. (De proprietatibus litterarum: series practica, 60)
4. *Phoenix: a Poetry Magazine*, edited by Harry Chambers. Nos. 11/12, Autumn and Winter 1973/4; Philip Larkin issue.
5. Timms, David. *Philip Larkin*. Edinburgh, Oliver & Boyd, 1973. Select bibliography pp. 132–8.

PARTS OF BOOKS

6. Allen, Walter. *Some Post-war British Writers*. [Stockholm], Sveriges radio, 1963. (pp. 90–102)
7. Alvarez, A. *Beyond all this Fiddle*. London, Penguin Press, 1968. (pp. 85–7)
8. Bedient, Calvin. *Eight Contemporary Poets*. London, Oxford University Press, 1974. (pp. 69–94)
9. Beloof, Robert. *The Performing Voice in Literature*. Boston, Little Brown, [c. 1961]. (Metrical criticism of "Wedding wind", pp. 436–7; critical examination of "Next, please", pp. 470–1)

10. Bold, Alan *ed. Cambridge Book of English Verse, 1939–1975.*
    Cambridge, Cambridge University Press, 1976. (Critical notes
    pp. 206–13)

11. Brewer, D. S. *Proteus: Studies in English Literature.* Tokyo,
    Kenkyusha, 1958. (pp. 233–61, esp. 253–7)

12. Cox, C. B. *and* Dyson, A. E. *Modern Poetry: Studies in Practical
    Criticism.* London, Arnold, 1963. ("At grass", pp. 137–41)

13. Danmarks Radio, Skoleradioen 1976. *Recent English Poetry,* [by]
    Edward Broadbridge. [Copenhagen], Danmarks Radio, 1976.
    (pp. 42–78)

14. Davie, Donald. *Thomas Hardy and British Poetry.* London,
    Routledge and Kegan Paul, 1973. (Landscapes of Larkin, pp. 63–
    82)

15. Enright, D. J. *Conspirators and Poets.* London, Chatto and Windus,
    1966. (Down cemetery road: the poetry of Philip Larkin, pp. 141–
    6. Originally published as a review of TWW.)

16. Falck, Colin. Philip Larkin. In *The Modern Poet: essays from 'The
    Review',* ed. by Ian Hamilton. London, Macdonald, 1968. (pp.
    101–10. Originally published as a review of TWW.)

17. Fraser, G. S. *Vision and Rhetoric : Studies in Modern Poetry.* London,
    Faber, 1959. (pp. 242–73)

18. Gindin, James. *Postwar British Fiction: New Accents and Attitudes.*
    London, Cambridge University Press; Berkeley, University of
    California Press, [c. 1962]. (Mainly chapter 1)

19. Grubb, Frederick. *A Vision of Reality: a Study of Liberalism in
    Twentieth-century Verse.* London, Chatto and Windus, 1965.
    (pp. 226–35)

20. Jennings, Elizabeth. *Poetry Today (1957–1960).* London, Long-
    mans for the British Council, 1961. (pp. 10–12)

21. Kleinstuck, Johannes. Philip Larkin "Church going". In *Die
    moderne englische Lyrik: Interpretationen,* ed. by Horst Oppel.
    Berlin, E. Schmidt Verlag, 1967. (pp. 295–302)

22. Moore, Geoffrey. *Poetry To-day.* London, Longmans for the
    British Council, 1958. (pp. 48–9)

23. O'Connor, William Van. *The New University Wits and the end
    of Modernism.* Carbondale, Southern Illinois University Press,
    1963. (pp. 16–29)

24. Rosenthal, M. L. *The Modern Poets: a Critical Introduction.* New
    York, Oxford University Press, 1960. (pp. 222–4)

25. ——. *The New Poets: American and British Poetry since World War*

II. New York, Oxford University Press, 1967. (pp. 233–44)

26. Sager, K. "Church going" and "Wedding wind". In *Criticism in Action*, ed. by Maurice Hussey. London, Longmans, 1969. (pp. 119–26)

27. Sinclair, J. McH. Taking a poem to pieces. In *Essays on Style and Language: Linguistic and Critical Approaches to Literary Style*, ed. by Roger Fowler. London, Routledge & Kegan Paul, 1966. (pp. 68–81).

28. Thurley, Geoffrey. *The Ironic Harvest: English Poetry in the Twentieth Century*. London, Arnold, 1974. (The legacy of Auden: the poetry of Roy Fuller, Philip Larkin and Peter Porter, pp. 137–62)

29. Thwaite, Anthony. *Contemporary English Poetry: an Introduction*. London, Heinemann, 1959. (pp. 148–50) [Originally entitled *Essays on Contemporary English Poetry* (Tokyo, Kenkyusha, 1957).]

30. ——. *Poetry Today, 1960–1970*. London, Longman for the British Council, 1973. (pp. 33–6)

31. ——. The poetry of Philip Larkin. In *The Survival of Poetry: a Contemporary Survey*, ed. by Martin Dodsworth. London, Faber, 1970. (pp. 37–55)

32. Wain, John. *Sprightly Running*. London, Macmillan, 1962. (pp. 187–8, *passim*)

33. Welz, Dieter. Larkin. In *Englische Literatur der Gegenwart*, ed. by Horst W. Drescher. Stuttgart, Kröner Verlag, [1970]. (pp. 581–9)

ARTICLES IN PERIODICALS

34. Alvarez, A. Stuff your pension! *Queen*, CCCCXXVI, 5594 (25 May 1966), 41–3.

35. Ball, Patricia. The photographic art. *Review of English Literature*, III (April 1962), 50–8.

36. Bateson, F. W. Auden's (and Empson's) heirs. *Essays in Criticism*, VII (January 1957), 76–80.

37. Blum, Margaret. Larkin's Dry-point. *Explicator*, XXXII, 6 (February 1974), item 48.

38. Brinnin, J. M. Young but not so angry. *Mademoiselle*, XLVI, 6 (April 1958), 150–1, 169–71.

39. Chambers, Harry. The poetry of Philip Larkin. *Phoenix*, 9 (Summer 1963), 30–6.

40. Cook, S. Modern Authors: 8, Philip Larkin. *School Librarian*, XXII (December 1974), 322–5.

41. Correspondence arising from the review of "The Whitsun weddings". *Cambridge Quarterly*, I (1966), 178–82.

42. Coulson, Michael. The sensibility angle: Philip Larkin. *Isis*, 1337 (4 February 1959), 11–14.

43. Cox, C. B. Philip Larkin. *Critical Quarterly*, I (Spring 1959), 14–17. (On "No road")

44. Cross, Colin. Poets and Their Worlds. *Observer* [colour supplement], 14 August 1966, pp. 10–17, 19.

45. Davie, Donald. Poetry and landscape in present [*sic*] England. *Granta*, LXVIII, 1229 (19 October 1963), 2–4.

46. Davison, Peter. The gilt edge of reputation: twelve months of new poetry. *Atlantic*, CCXVII (January 1966), 82–5.

47. Dodsworth, Martin. The climate of pain in recent English poetry. *London Magazine*, n.s. IV, 6 (November 1964), 86–92.

48. Faulkner, Peter. Philip Larkin: a poet of our world. *Humanist*, 84 (May 1969), 145–7.

49. Ferguson, Peter. Philip Larkin's *XX Poems*: the missing link. *Agenda*, XIV, 3 (Autumn 1976), 53–65.

50. Fraser, G. S. English poetry in the 1950s. *Audience*, VIII, 2 (Spring 1961), 42–57. (Quotes entire "Coming" and "Lines on a young lady's photograph album".)

51. Gardner, Philip. The wintry drum: the poetry of Philip Larkin. *Dalhousie Review*, XLVIII, 1 (September 1968), 88–99.

52. Goode, J. A reading of "Deceptions". *Tamesis* [University of Reading], Summer 1961, pp. 4–8.

53. Greenfield, Stanley B. Grammar and meaning in poetry. *PMLA*, LXXXII, 5 (October 1967), 377–87.

54. Hainsworth, J. D. A poet of our time. *Hibbert Journal*, LXIV, 255 (Midsummer 1966), 153–5.

55. Hall, Donald. A note on this issue. *Michigan Quarterly Review*, IX, 3 (Summer 1970), 145.

56. Hamilton, Ian. The making of the Movement. *New Statesman*, LXXXI, 2092 (23 April 1971), 570–1.

57. ——. Greek street. Larkin: a text restored. *The New Review*, I, 4 (July 1974), 3. (On "Going, going".)

58. John, Noel. Some poems of Philip Larkin. *Humberside*, XVI, 3 (Autumn 1970), 3–17.

59. Jones, Alun. The poetry of Philip Larkin: a note on transatlantic

culture. *Western Humanities Review*, XVI, 2 (Spring 1962), 143–52.

60. Lambourne, David. Outside the window. *Torch* [University of Hull], [June] 1965, pp. 3–6.

61. Lehmann, John. The Wain-Larkin myth. *Sewanee Review*, LXVI, 4 (Autumn 1958), 578–87.

62. McCoola, R. Philip Larkin. *Grapevine* [University of Durham Institute of Education], IV (February 1957), 7. (On the poem "Success story" reprinted here in full.)

63. McIntyre, John P. Radical imperfection: the poetry of Philip Larkin. *Month*, 2nd series IX, 9 (September 1976), 313–17.

64. Milligan, I. Philip Larkin's "The Whitsun weddings" and Virginia Woolf's "The waves". *Notes and Queries*, n.s. XXIII, 1 (January 1976), 23.

65. Morrison, Blake. The Movement: a re-assessment. *PN review*, IV, 1 ([November] 1976), 26–9.

66. Murphy, Richard. Three modern poets. *Listener*, LIV, 1384 (8 September 1955), 373–5.

67. Naremore, James. Philip Larkin's "lost world". *Contemporary Literature*, XV, 3 (Summer 1974), 331–44.

68. Oberg, Arthur. Larkin's lark eggs: the vision is sentimental. *Stand*, XVIII, 1 ([December]1976), 21–6.

69. O'Connor, William Van. The new university wits. *Kenyon Review*, XX, 1 (Winter 1958), 38–50. (Quotes "Wants" entire.)

70. Page, Norman. Philip Larkin's "Myxomatosis": a critical appreciation. *Critical Survey*, II, 3 (Winter 1965), 169–70.

71. Parkinson, R. N. 'To keep our metaphysics warm': a study of "Church going" by Philip Larkin. *Critical Survey*, V, 3 (Winter 1971), 224–33.

72. Peschmann, Hermann. Philip Larkin: laureate of the common man. *English*, XXIV, 119 (Summer 1975), 49–58.

73. Press, John. English verse since 1945. *Essays by Divers Hands*, n.s. XXXI (1962), 143–84.

74. Ricks, Christopher. The words and music of life. *Sunday Times*, 7 January 1968, p. 39. (Reprints and discusses "Love songs in age".)

75. Robinson, James K. Terror lumped and split: contemporary British and American poets. *Southern Review*, n.s. VI, 1 (January 1970), 216–28.

76. Roper, Derek. Tradition and innovation in the Occidental lyric of the lost decade. I: English poetry and the tradition, 1950–1960. *Books Abroad*, XXXIV, 4 (Autumn 1960), 344–8.

77. Spender, Stephen. The present position of poetic writing in England. *Cairo Studies in English*, 1961/62, pp. 8–15.

78. Stock, Noel. Lowell and Larkin. *Poetry Australia*, 54 (1975), 74–9.

79. Swinden, Patrick. Old lines, new lines: the Movement ten years after. *Critical Quarterly*, IX, 4 (Winter 1967), 347–59.

80. Thwaite, Anthony *and* Silkin, Jon. No politics, no poetry? *Stand*, VI, 2 (1963), 7–23.

81. Tomlinson, Charles. The middlebrow muse. *Essays in Criticism*, VII (January 1957), 208–17.

82. Ure, Peter. Philip Larkin [letter]. *Critical Quarterly*, VI, 3 (Autumn 1964), 277–8.

83. Wain, John. Engagement or withdrawal? Some notes on the work of Philip Larkin. *Critical Quarterly*, VI, 2 (Summer 1964), 167–78. (A correction is made on pp. 277–8.)

84. ——. English poetry: the immediate situation. *Sewanee Review*, LXV, 3 (Summer 1957), 353–74. (Quotes entire "Maiden name", "Referred back" and "Church going".)

85. Watson, J. R. The other Larkin. *Critical Quarterly*, XVII, 4 (Winter 1975), 347–60.

86. Weatherhead, A. K. Philip Larkin of England. *ELH*, XXXVIII, 4 (December 1971), 616–30.

87. Weiss, Theodore. Philip Larkin's antidote. *Poetry Dimension*, 4 (1976), 87–95.

88. Welz, Dieter. "A winter landscape in neutral colours": some notes on Philip Larkin's vision of reality. *Theoria* [Pietermaritzburg], XXXIX (October 1972), 61–73.

89. Wesling, Donald. The inevitable ear . . . *ELH*, XXXVI, 3 (September 1969), 544–61.

90. Wiseman, Christopher. Poetic limits: an assessment of Philip Larkin. *Glasgow Review*, I, 2 (Summer 1964), 19–22.

THESES AND ACADEMIC DISSERTATIONS

91. Ackroyd, Nicki Sahlin. The poetry of Philip Larkin. M.A., Brown University, 1971.

92. Jackson, Judith Anne. The development of Philip Larkin's poetry. M.A., North Dakota State University, 1965.

93. Kuby, Lolette Beth. Philip Larkin's poetry. Ph.D., Case Western Reserve University, 1970.

94. Rigal, Denis. Le Mouvement et la poésie de Ph. Larkin. Thèse de doctorat, Université de Bretagne Occidentale, 1975.

95. Robinson, M. And now we have the Movement, mostly still: a group of contemporary British poets; R. S. Thomas, Philip Larkin, Thom Gunn and Ted Hughes. Ph.D., University of Exeter, 1965.

96. Sola Buil, Ricardo. La actitud poética de Philip Larkin, Ted Hughes y Thom Gunn. M.A., Zaragoza University, 1972.

INDEX

References in this index are to item numbers in the bibliography. The titles of Larkin's works are capitalized. The titles of books which Larkin reviewed, the titles of periodicals publishing reviews of his work, and the titles of critical studies are not indexed. Titles like "Poem", "Song", or "Sonnet" are not indexed unless a work is definitely known by that title. Initial definite and indefinite articles are inverted in alphabetization; "*n*" indicates a reference to a foot- or headnote.

A. C. Benson Silver Medal, C444
About twenty years ago, A7, C196, F3, K5
ABOVE 80° N, A1, K5
Abse, Dannie, L4, L31
ABSENCES, A6, B6, F1, F7
ABSTRACT VISION, C57
Ackroyd, Nicki Sahlin, App. 91
Adventures with the Irish Brigade, B17
AFTER THE MODERNS, A8, C170
AFTERNOONS, A7, C121, F3, K4
AGE, A6, C43, F1, F7, K5
Albertson, C., C422
ALIVE AND WELL, C372
ALIVE FROM NEW ORLEANS, A8, C251
All catches alight, A1, B2, K13
All I remember is, A1
ALL WHAT JAZZ, A8, L25
Allen, W. C. *and* Rust, B. A. L., C90
Allen, Walter, App. 6
Allison, J., C157
Allott, Kenneth, L12
Alvarez, A., A7a, App. 7, App. 34
Always too eager for the future, we, A4, A6, B3, C48, F1, F5, F7, K13, App. 9
AMAZING ARMSTRONG, A8, C324
AMBASSADOR EXTRAORDINARY, A8, C199

AMBASSADOR JAZZ, A8, C199
AMBULANCES, A7, C139, C156, C275, F3, L13, L15, L16
Amis, Kingsley, A3a, A4, A8a, A10a, C69a, H*n*
Amis, Martin, A3e
Amis, Sally, A6, C44
AMONG THE DUCAL PORTRAITS, C392
And if she were to admit, A1
And the walker sees the sunlit battle-field, C17
ANNUS MIRABILIS, A10, C301, C348, C362, F6
Antaeus, C429, H9
Antiquarian Book Fair, 1972, B11
APOLLO BIT, THE, C312
Arabesque, C27
Ardizzone, Edward, F6
ARETHA'S GOSPEL, A8, C314
Argo records, F6
Ark, C67
ARMSTRONG OUT ON HIS OWN, C339
ARMSTRONG TO PARKER, A8, C173
ARMSTRONG'S LAST GOOD-NIGHT, C387
ARRIVAL, A4
ARRIVALS, DEPARTURES, A5, A6, C53, F1, F7, K5, K13
ARTICULATE DEVOTION, C428

Arts Book Society *see* Readers Union
    Arts Book Society
*Arts Council collection of modern literary
    manuscripts, 1963–1972, The*, B15
Arts Council of Great Britain, The,
    B7, B15, F6
ARUNDEL TOMB, AN, A7, C58, C69,
    C75, F2, F3, F7, G7, K13, L5, L6,
    L9, L16
AS BAD [GOOD] AS A MILE, A7, C137,
    C216, F3
AS IT WAS IN THE GOOD OLD DAYS,
    A8, C217
ASK ME NOW, A8, C243
AT FIRST, A7, C64, E1, F3, K5, L7
AT GRASS, A4, A5, A6, B3, B5, C394,
    F1, F7, G18, K13, App. 12
At last you yielded up the album, A5,
    A6, C53, F1, F7, K13, L3, L12,
    App. 50
At once whatever happened starts
    receding, A5, A6, F1, K7
At one the wind rose, A1, K13
Atlantic, C156
ATMOSPHERIC PRESSURE, A8, C214
Auden, W. H., B12, C60, C129, C427
Audit, C137
Australian letters, C108

Baddeley, V. C. Clinton- *see* Clinton-
    Baddeley, V. C.
BAFFLING SAX AND BAROQUE
    PIANO, A8, C243
Bailey, J. O., C86
Balkite, The, C186
Ball, Patricia, App. 35
Balliett, Whitney, C132, C231, C306
BANDS ACROSS THE SEA, A8, C141
Barnes, William, C178
BASIE AT HIS BEST, A8, C276
BASIE: THE FIRST AND BEST, A8,
    C276
Bateson, F. W., A6a, App. 36

BATTLE WITHOUT CONFLICT, A8,
    C207
Bayley, John, A10a, C78
Baylis, Ebenezer, and Son Ltd., B8
Bechet, Sidney, A7, C122, F3, K13
BECHET AND BIRD, A8, C142
Bedient, Calvin, A10b, B12, App. 8
Beer, Patricia, L15
BEFORE TEA, A7, C121, F3, K4
Bell, William, B2
Beloit Poetry Journal, C85
Beloof, Robert, App. 9
BENNY'S IMMORTAL HOUR, A8,
    C138
Benson, A. C. Silver Medal, C444
Bergonzi, Bernard, A2c, B12
Berry, Francis, C167
Berryman, John, C106
BERTRAND RUSSELL AND D. H.
    LAWRENCE, C31
BESSIE AND BILLIE, C422
BESSIE SMITH STORY [ALONE], THE,
    A8, C263
Best Poems of 1956, L6
Betjeman, Sir John, A7a, B9, C54,
    C99, C103, C135, C187, C390,
    C411, C424, C426, G13, G17,
    G29, App. 87
BETTER THAN THE BEST, A8, C142
Beverley Grammar School, E20
Beverlonian, The, E20
BEYOND A JOKE, C54
Beyond all this, the wish to be alone,
    A4, A6, C163, C394, F1, F4, F7,
    K1, K4, K13, L1, L14
BIG FELLERS, THE, A8, C258
BIG NOISE FROM YESTERDAY, A8,
    C179
BIG VICTIMS, C353
BILLIE'S GOLDEN YEARS, A8, C184
BILLY BANKS SIDES, THE, A8, C219
Binyon, Michael, E17
BIRDLIFE, C423

Birkenhead, Earl of, B9
Black paper two, H7
Blackburn, Thomas, L5
Blackwell, Basil & Mott, B1
BLENDING OF BETJEMAN, THE, C135
BLIZZARD, A1, K5
BLOWING BRITISH, A8, C307
Blum, Margaret, App. 37
Blunden, Edmund, A1c
Bogan, Louise, A6b, A7b
Bold, Alan, A2d, A3d, J6, App. 10
BOLD BAD BEAUTY, C91
BOND'S LAST CASE, C273
Booker, Christopher, A8a
BOOKS OF THE YEAR, C397, C437, C446, C449
BOP-MASTER BROWN, A8, C281
Borestone Mountain poetry awards 1957, L6
BORN YESTERDAY, A6, C44, F1, L3
Bott, C., A2d, A3d
Bottle is drunk out one by one, The, A1, B2, C110, K5
Bowen, J., A2c
Bowering Press, The, A1c, A7a, A7d, A10a
Bowman, Derek, A10a
Box of teak, a box of sandalwood, A, C28
Boyle, Harris, H8
Boys dream of native girls who bring breadfruit, C152
BREADFRUIT, C152
Brett, R. L., B12, H16
Brewer, D. S., App. 11
Brinnin, J. M., App. 38
British Broadcasting Corporation, F9–11, F14–17, G *passim*
British Council, F4, F6, F12
British Museum, B7
Broadbridge, Edward, App. 13
BROADCAST, A7, C164, F3

Brooke, Jocelyn, C198
Brooke, Rupert, C312
Brown, S., A8a
Brownjohn, Alan, A10a, L27, App. 1
Brunn, H. O., C174
Bryce, N., A8a
BRYNMOR JONES LIBRARY, THE, D *passim*, H6
BUBBLES WALLER BLEW, THE, A8, C271
Buil, Ricardo Sola *see* Sola Buil, Ricardo
BUILDING, THE, A10, C402, F6, L30
Burgess, Anthony, G13
Burn, James, B4
BURSTING-OUT OF THE BLUES, C354
But we must build our walls, for what we are, C19
By the tide of Humber, L26
BYWAYS OF THE BLUES, C318

CALLING THE TUNE, C432
Campbell, Roy, C119
CAN THE REAL THING COME ALONG ANY MORE?, A8, C278
Canadian Broadcasting Corporation, F8, G9
CARD-PLAYERS, THE, A10, C368, F6
Carey, John, A1c
CARNIVAL IN VENICE, C123
Carswell's [printers] of Belfast, A4
Caught in the centre of a soundless field, A6, C45, F1, K9, App. 70
Causley, Charles, C79
Chambers, Harry, A6a, A7a, App. 4, App. 39
Cherwell, C20, C21, C22, C26
CHOSEN AND RECOMMENDED, C66
CHURCH GOING, A6, C56, F1, F7, G18, K1, K11, K13, K16, L3, L12, L22, App. 21, App. 26, App. 71, App. 84.

Churchill, R. C., C198

Ciardi, John, A6b

Clarendon Press, B12

Clark, C., A8b

Clay, Richard, Ltd., B12

Clayton, Peter, A8a, C267

Cleanliness is next to?, C10

Climbing the hill within the deafening wind, A1, K13

Clinton-Baddeley, V. C., F2

Closed like confessionals, they thread, A7, C139, C156, C275, F3, L13, L15, L16

Coleman, John, A2b

Collected Poems [of John Betjeman], enlarged edition, B9

COLOUR OF THEIR MUSIC, THE, C356

Come to sunny Prestatyn, A7, C194, F3

COMING, A4, A6, F1, F4, F7, K2, K5, L1, App. 50

Coming up England by a different line, A6, C52, F1, F7, K13, L3, L21

Condon, Eddie, C81

CONFIDENCE OF COLEMAN, THE, A8, C288

Connell, John, A2b

Connolly, Cyril, B12

Conquest, Robert, Hn, L3, L17

CONSCRIPT, A1, C23

CONTINUING TO LIVE, B14

Continuing to live—that is, repeat, B14

CONTRASTING EQUALS, A8, C173

Cook, S., App. 40

Cook, W., C350

COOL BRITANNIA, A8, C145

COOL LOOK AT BIRD, A, A8, C210

COPYRIGHT OF LETTERS, C355, C357

Corke, Hilary, L11

Cornhill, C390

Cotton, John, A5

Coulson, Michael. App. 42

Coventrian, The, C1–18

Coventry Evening Telegraph, E15

Cover, C301

Cox, C.B., A10a, B5, H7, L16, L18–20, L22, App. 12, App. 43

CREDO, A8, C285

Crispin, Edmund, A2b, H2, *see also* Montgomery, Bruce

CRITIC AMONG ELUSIVE LABELS, C331

CRITIC AS HIPSTER, THE, C132

Critical Quarterly, B5, C114, C133, C152, C171, C269, C270, L16, L18–20, L22

Critical quarterly society, H7, L22, L29

CRITICS' CHOICE, C159

Cross, Collin, App. 44

CULTS AND CRITICISM, A8, C261

Cuming, Agnes, C172A

CURLING UP WITH A GOOD RECORD, C330

Curtis, Anthony, A2b, A7a

CUT GRASS, A10, C385, F6

Cut grass lies frail, A10, C385, F6

Daily Telegraph, C136, C138, C140–2, C145–7, C151, C153, C158, C160, C162, C168, C170, C172, C173, C175–7, C179, C184, C188, C191, C192, C195, C199, C203–7, C210, C211, C213, C214, C217, C218, C219, C222, C225, C227, C228, C230, C232–40, C242, C243, C245–7, C249, C251–3, C255, C256, C258–61, C263, C264, C266, C271, C274, C276, C278, C279, C281, C282, C285–9, C291, C294, C295, C297, C299, C300, C302, C303, C307, C309, C311, C314, C316, C319, C322–4, C326–8,

C331, C333, C336–9, C341, C343–7, C349, C351, C354, C356, C358, C360, C363, C364, C367, C369, C370, C372–4, C376, C379–82, C384, C387, C388, C392, C396, C403, C432, C433, F3, *see also Weekend Telegraph*
Dale, Peter, A7a
DANCER, THE, A1
Dartmouth, Countess of, B10
Davie, Donald, B12, C116, C167, App. 14, App. 45
Davie, Ian, B1
Davies, W. H., C201
DAVIS DECLAIMED, A8, C258
Davison, Peter, App. 46
DAWN, A1
Day, Roger, App. 2
Day Lewis, Cecil, B7, C126, C212, C359, C365, L5
DAYS, A7, C82, C89, C394, F3, F4, F5, G18, K5
DEAR OLD DIXIE, A8, C309
DEATH OF THE BLUES, THE, A8, C205
DECEPTIONS, A4, A6, B3, F1, F7, K1, K13, L1, App. 52
DECLINE OF NIGHT-MUSIC, A8, C228
DECLINING NIGHT MUSIC, A8, C228
DEDICATED, THE, A4
Deen, R. F., A7b
De La Mare, Walter, C353
Delaunay, C., C154
Dell Publishing Co., B6
DELVING INTO THE PAST, A8, C299
Dennis, Nigel, B12
Departure, C48, C50, C70
Derleth, August, A6b
Derwent College, University of York, E12
Dezső, Tandori, K8
Deutsch, Babette, C78

Dial Press, The, B6
Dickinson, Emily, C353
Dickinson, Patric, L2
Difficult part of love, The, C269
DISAGREEABLE TO UNBEARABLE, C290
DISINTEGRATION, C25
DISTANT PROSPECTS, C30
DIXIELAND BAG, THE, A8, C253
DIXIELAND BAND, THE, A8, C309
DIXIELAND ROLLED INTO ONE, A8, C253
DJANGO LIFE, THE, A8, C259
DO STUDIOS KILL?, A8, C214
Dobrée, Bonamy, B4
DOCKERY AND SON, A7, C202, F3, F4, K13, L19
Dockery was junior to you, A7, C202, F3, F4, K13, L19
DOCUMENTER OF JAZZ, THE, A8, C266
Dodsworth, Martin, App. 32, App. 47
DOMINANT COME-LATELY, A8, C197
Donoghue, Dennis, B12
DON'T GO 'WAY NOBODY, A8, C191
Dorn, N. K., A6b
DOWN AMONG THE DEAD MEN, C114
Down cemetery road, G13
Down stucco sidestreets, A10, C368, F6, K2, K15
Drescher, Horst W., App. 33
Drewery, Robert Forrester, C320
DRY-POINT, A4, A6, F1, App. 37
DUBLINESQUE, A10, C368, F6, K2, K15
DUCAL MYSTIQUE, THE, A8, C286
Duncan, Frances Ross, B14
Dunn, Douglas, H9
Durham, University Institute of Education *see* University of Durham Institute of Education

Dutton, Geoffrey, C108
Dyson, A. E. B5, H7, L16, L18–20, L22, App. 12

Eagleton, Terry, A10a
Eboracum, E12
ECHOES OF THE GATSBY ERA, A8, C136
Edmands, Robert, E11
Eells, G., C293
Ego's county he inherited, The, A1, C23
ELLINGTON MINUS THE DUKE, A8, C168
ELLINGTON PANORAMA, A8, C217
ELLINGTON REPUTATION, THE, A8, C286
Ellison, R., C284
Encounter, C109, C368, C424, C431, C439
END OF A SWINGING ERA, THE, A8, C266
END OF JAZZ, THE, A8, C205
Endlessly, time-honoured irritant, A4, A6, F1, App. 37
Engle, Paul, B6
English Poetry Now, L16
Enright, D. J., A4, A7a, B3, App. 15
Essays in Criticism, C36
ESSENTIAL BEAUTY, A7, C183, C186, F3
ETCHING, A4
Europa Hotel, B11
Evans, Barbara Lloyd, L21
Even so distant I can taste the grief, A4, A6, B3, F1, F7, K1, K13, L1, App. 52
Ewart, Gavin, H*n*
EXHUMATION, C126
EXPECTATIONS KEEP REPUTATIONS ALIVE, C344
EXPLOSION, THE A9, A10, C410, F6

Eye can hardly pick them out, The, A4, A5, A6, B3, B5, C394, F1, F7 G18, K13, App. 12
Ezra Pound: the critical heritage, L28

Faber & Faber, A1c–d, A2b, d, A3a, c, d, A7a, d, A8a, A10a, B8
FACT AND FICTION, A8, C177
FAITH HEALING, A7, C130, C161, F3, K13, L11
Falck, Colin, A7a, App. 16
FANTASY POETS, No. 21, A5
Fantasy Press, A5
FAR FROM DIFFERENT GUY, A, A8, C259
Farncombe & Co., A2a
Farrar, Straus & Giroux, A10b
FAST AND HIGH, A8, C249
FATS WALLER AND HIS FORMULA, A8, C271
Faulkner, Peter, App. 48
FEARS OF THE BRAVE, C6
Feather, Leonard, C101
Ferguson, Peter, App. 49
FICTION AND THE READING PUBLIC, C36, G4
FIFTY YEARS BACK, C16
FIRST SIGHT, A7, C64, E1, F3, K5, L7
Fleming, Ian, C273
Fletcher, Iain, L1
FLUTE BETWEEN TWO WAVES, A8, C274
FOLK HEROES IN BOWLERS, A8, C145
Folkways records, F2
For nations vague as weed, A7, C165, F3, F4
FOR SIDNEY BECHET, A7, C67, C180, F3, K5, K13, L17
Forget-me-not lane, L25
FORGET WHAT DID, A10, F6
Fortune Press, The, A1a–b, A2a, B2
FORTUNE TELLING, A1, K5

Four, L22
Fowler, Roger, App. 27
Fox, C., A8a
Fox, Robert, F13, G20
FRAGMENT FROM MAY, C7
FRAGMENTS OF A GOLDEN AGE, C358
Fraser, G. S., A6a, L1, App. 17, App. 50
Freedland, M., C432
Freeman, Ruth Welland- *see* Welland-Freeman, Ruth
FRESHLY SCRUBBED POTATO, C201
FRIDAY NIGHT IN THE ROYAL STATION HOTEL, A10, C283, C321, F6
FRIVOLOUS AND VULNERABLE, C182, H6
FROM CLIFFORD TO CONNIE, A8, C281
FROM CLUBS TO CONCERTS, A8, C235
FROM THE FESTIVAL PLATFORMS, A8, C239
FROM TRAD TO THE OTHER THING, C384
Fuller, Roy, A6a
FUNNY HAT MEN, THE, A8, C287
FUNNY OLD HAT, A8, C287

Gammond, Peter, C91, C93, C267
GARDEN IS A LOVESOME THING, A, C4
Gardner, Philip, A10, App. 51
Gardner, Raymond, E16
George, Daniel *pseud.*, A3a
GETTING THE GIGS, C448
GETTING UP IN THE MORNING, C1
Ghose, Zulfikar, A7a
Giant whispering and coughing from, A7, C164, F3
Gibson, James, B13
Gindin, James, App. 18

GIRL IN WINTER, A, A3, K3, K17
Gittings, R., C440
Give me a thrill, says the reader, C36, G4
GIVING THE BIRD TO THE LEGEND, A8, C246
GLEANINGS FROM A POOR YEAR FOR POETRY, C124
Godbolt, J., C448
Goff, Martyn, H3
GOING, A4, A6, B3, C394, F1, F7, K2, K4, K5, L14, L21
GOING, GOING, A10, B10, C406, F6
GOING MORE CHROMATIC THAN POP, C343
Goode, J., App. 52
GOODMAN'S GUITAR MAN, A8, C279
Goreau, A., C448
Gottlieb, G., A3b
Gownsman *pseud.*, E3
GRACE NOTES FROM OUTER SPACE, A8, C176
Graham, D., A10a
Grant, Damian, L29
Grapevine, The, C72
Graves, Robert, C98, C106, G8
GREAT RUSSELL BAND, THE, A8, C291
Green, Benny, C181
Green Ginger, E18
Green-shadowed people sit, or walk in rings, A4, A6, F1, K5, K9
Greenfield, Stanley B., App. 53
Grey day for the Show, but cars jam the narrow lanes, A10, C431, F6
Grigson, Geoffrey, C332, C428
Gröndahl, Britta, K16
Groping back to bed after a piss, A10, C313, F6, K2, K8
Grossman, W. L. *and* Farrell, J. W., C96
GROUPINGS, C198

GROWTH OF THE BLUES, THE, A8,
    C140
GRUB VALE, C350
Grubb, F., App. 19
Guardian, C113, C116, C118, C119,
    C122, C124, C128, C132, C154,
    C157, C159, C208, C248, C257,
    C267, C272, C277, C284, C290,
    C293, C306, C318, C332, C340,
    C342, C350, C393, C414, C448,
    E7, E16, for previous entries *see
    Manchester Guardian*
Guinness Book of Poetry, L7, L8, L10,
    L13
GUITARIST TO GOODMAN, A8, C279
GULLIVER'S TRAVAILS, C284
Gunner, Colin C., B17

Haddon Craftsmen, B6
Hainsworth, J. D., App. 54
Hajnal, Anna, K7
Hall, Donald, A6b, App. 55
Hall, J. C., L2
Hall, Julian, *The Senior Commoner*, A2a
Hambledon, Ronald, F8, G9
Hamblett, Charles, J1
Hamburger, Michael, J2
Hamilton, Ian, A7a, B12, E5, H9, I2,
    J5, App. 56, App. 57
Hamilton, Steuart, E20
Hancox, Alan, I2, J3, J5
HAND AND FLOWER PRESS, C35
HANDBOOK FOR HEADS OF
    DEPARTMENTS, D8
HAPPY FIELDS, C13
Hardy, Emma, C171, C405
Hardy, Thomas, C315, C440, F14
HARDY'S MIND AND HEART, C381
Harrap, George C. & Co., B13
HARSH AND BITTER-SWEET, C90
Hartley, Anthony, A5, A6a
Hartley, George, A6a, c, A10a, F1, F3
HAVING A BALL, A8, C138

HEADS IN THE WOMEN'S WARDS,
    C404
Heaney, Seamus, L27
Heath-Stubbs, John, C40
Heaviest of flowers, the head, A1, B2
Hentoff, Nat *and* MacCarthy, A.,
    C132
Her hands intend no harm, C28
Her Majesty's Stationery Office, B10
HERE, A7, C155, F3, F5, H10, H16,
    K4, K13, L23, L26
HIDDEN HARDY, THE, C405
Higgins, Brian, H*n*
HIGH WINDOWS, A10, F6, G25
Higher than the handsomest hotel,
    A10, C402, F6, L30
Higson, Norman, C389
Hill, Frances, E13
Hill, Susan, A2b
Hill, W. B., A2c
Hilliard, S. S., A10b
HISTORY, A10, C301, C348, C362
Hodgson, Ralph, C115
Hobsbawm, Philip, A7a
Hobson, H., A7b
Hoggart, Richard, A6a
Holiday, Billie, C90
Holiday, Billie *and* Dufty, W., C422
HOLIDAY IN SPRING AND SUMMER,
    A8, C184
Holland, Mary, E9
Holloway, David, F3
Holloway, John, A7a, C79
HOLY GROWL, THE, A8, C203
HOMAGE TO A GOVERNMENT, A10,
    C329, F6
HOME FIRES BURNING, A8, C307
HOME IS SO SAD, A7, C220, F3, G22,
    K13
Hope, Francis, A2b, A7a
Horder, John, E7
HORN IN [OF] A DILEMMA, A8, C158
Horns of the morning, The, A1, B2

Horrocks, R., C81, C111
HOTTEST RECORD EVER MADE, THE, A8, C303
Hough, Graham, A6a
Houghton Mifflin Co., B9
HOUNDED, C117
HOW, C366
HOW AM I TO KNOW?, A8, C261
HOW BILLIE SCORES, A8, C256
HOW DISTANT, A10, C296, F6, L24
How distant, the departures of young men, A10, C296, F6, L24
HOW DO WE STAND, A8, C235
How do you want to live?, B10
How high they build hospitals, C366
HOW LONG HAS THIS BEEN GOING ON, A8, C324
HOW RUSHING WENT ON SINGING, A8, 294
Howden, J., G25
Hugh-Jones, Siriol, A2b
Hughes, B. N., C18
Hughes, Ted, L15
Hull Printers, A8a
Humberside, C65, C94, C321, C391
Hurrying to catch my Comet, A7, C143, C229, F3
Hussey, Maurice, App. 27

I deal with farmers, things like dips and feeds, A10, C400, F6, L29
I dreamed of an out-thrust [out-stretched] arm of land, A1, B1, C27, K5, K13
I put my mouth, A1, B2, F5
I REMEMBER, I REMEMBER, A6, C52, F1, F7, K13, L3, L21
I saw three ships go sailing by, A1, K5, K13
I see a girl dragged by the wrists, A1, B2, C110
I thought it would last my time, A10, B10, C406, F6

I will climb thirty steps to my room, A1
IDOLS OF THE TWENTIES, A8, C255
If grief could burn out, A1
If hands could free you, heart, A1, K5, K13
If I were called in, A7, C82, C89, C394, F3, L17
If my darling were once to decide, A4, A5, A6, B3, C49, F1, F7, G3, K9, L14
IGNORANCE, A7, C61, F3
Ikio, Kanaseki, K11
I'M COMING! BEWARE OF ME, A8, C302
IMAGINARY MUSEUM PIECE, C116
IMPORTANCE OF ELSEWHERE, THE, A7, C51, C65, C87, F3
IN BENNY GOODMAN'S GOLDEN DAYS, C403
In frames as large as rooms that face all ways, A7, C183, C186, F3
In the field, two horses, A1, C394, K5, K13
IN THE FRONT SEAT, A8, C291
IN THE GRIP OF LIGHT, I1
IN THE MAINSTREAM MANNER, A8, C295
IN WHITE TIE AND TAILS, C379
INCOMPARABLE MAX, THE, C238
INIMITABLE JIMMY YANCEY, THE, A8, C316
"Interesting, but futile", said his diary, C21
Is it for now or for always, A1, K5, K13
IT COULD ONLY HAPPEN IN ENGLAND, B9, C390, L31

Jackson, Judith Anne, App. 92
Jackson, N., C250
Jacobson, Dan, E19

Jake Balowsky, my biographer, A10, C313, F6

JAM YESTERDAY, A8, C188

James, Clive, A2d, A3d, A8a, A10a, F6, H13

Jan van Hogspeuw staggers to the door, A10, C368, F6

JAZZ AS A WAY OF LIFE, A8, C177

JAZZ-MAN'S SOUND AND FURY, C388

JAZZMEN, C292

JAZZ RECORDS OF THE YEAR, C160

Jennings, Elizabeth, A1c, A2b, A7a, A10a, C92, L4, App. 20

Jennings, S. C., & Son, A1

Jewell, Derek, A8a

JILL, A2, I3

John Roberts Press Ltd., A9, B14, B16

Jones, Alan Pryce- see, Pryce-Jones, Alan

Jones, Alun, App. 59

Jones, David, F4

Jones, L., C342

Jones, M. and Chilton, J., C393

Jones, Monica, A6

Jones, Siriol Hugh-, see Hugh-Jones, Siriol

Joseph, Michael, B4

Journal of Documentation, C401

Jupiter Anthology of Twentieth Century English Poetry, part III, F2

JUST A LITTLE WHILE, C328

JUST AROUND THE CORNER, C346

K.H.S. IN BRUSSELS, EASTER 1939, C15

Kaminsky, Max, C 238

Kavanagh, P. J., C116

Keene, D., A6a,

Keepsake, A, B14

Keil, C., C277

Kenkyusha Ltd., B3

Kennelly, B., A7a

Kenner, Hugh, C63

Kermode, Frank, C80

Kick up the fire, and let the flames break loose, A1, K13

Kinsella, Thomas, A7b

Kirkeby, E., C272

Kleinstuck, Johannes, App. 21

Knole Park Press, A1b

Kuby, Lolette, App. 3, App. 93

Kustow, Michael, Hn

Lambourne, David, App. 60

Lambs that learn to walk in snow, A7, C64, E1, F3, K5, L7

Lancaster, Osbert, F2

Langbaum, R., C80

Langland, Joseph, B6

Langridge, Derek, C371

LARGE COOL STORE, THE, A7, C144, F3, K13

Larkin at 50, F16, G23

Larkinland, Hn

LAST-BUT-ONE-ROUND-UP, C128

Latest face, so effortless, A4, A6, C38, F1, L3

Latimer Trend & Co., A2b, A3c

LAYING DOWN LIGHT FICTION, C322

Leach, J. R., A1b

LEGEND, A1, K5

LEGEND OF THE JUNGLE, A8, C203

Lehmann, John, App. 61

Leonard, N., C200

LESS DECEIVED, THE, A6, B3, F1, K10

Let the poet choose, B13

Levenson, Christopher, A6a

Levi, Peter, C124

Lewis, Cecil Day see Day Lewis, Cecil

Lewis, Jenny see Stratford, Jenny

Lewis, Naomi, A6a

LIBRARY AND THE DEPARTMENTS, THE, D12

Library Association record, C29, C127, C172a, C371, C413

LICE, FLEAS AND GULLIBLE MAYFLIES, C118

LIFE WITH A HOLE IN IT, THE, B16, L32

Light spreads darkly downwards from the high, A10, C283, C321, F6

Like the train's best, A1, C110

LINES ON A YOUNG LADY'S PHOTOGRAPH ALBUM, A5, A6, C53, F1, F7, K13, L3, L12, App. 50

Lipton, L., C123

Listen, C42, C46, C55, C60, C61, C74, C82, C83, C87, C103, C121, C180, F1, F3

Listener, C19, C35, C51, C130, C164, C174, C178, C202, C212, C215, C216, C220, C226, C296, C315, C385, C410, C416, C418, C419, C421, E14, G13

LISTENING WITH A DIFFERENCE, C367

LITTLE NIGHT MUSIC, A, A8, C245

LIVES OF THE POETS, C154

LIVINGS, A10, C400, F6, L29

LLOYD DOES SOMETHING PRETTY A8, C278

Locke, D., A8a

Logue, Christopher, C83, C106

Lomax, Alan, C238

London Magazine, C58, C59, C77, C165, C166, C194, C298, C348, E5, I2, J7

London University *see* University of London

Lonely in Ireland, since it was not home, A7, C51, C65, C87, F3

LOOK NO KANGAROOS, C108

LOOKING AT PARKER, A8, C210

LOOKING BACK AT COLTRANE, A8

LOOKING BACK AT LOUIS, A8, C153

LOOKING BACK AT LYTTELTON, C363

LOSS TO JAZZ, A, A8, C274

LOVE, C269

LOVE SONGS IN AGE, A7, B5, F3, K5, K13, L10, L17, App. 74

Love we must part now: do not let it be, A1, B2, K5, K13

LOVELY GIGS, C257

Lowell, Robert, B12, C106

Luciad, C30

LUCKY OLD ENGLAND'S POET, C411

Lyttelton, Humphrey, C93

Mabon, C335, K17

MacBeth, George, A5

McCoola, R., App. 62

MacDonagh, D. *and* Robinson, L., C100

McIntyre, John P., App. 63

MacLeish, Archibald, C401

MacNamara, E., A3b

MacNeice, Louis, B4, C79, C209

McRae, B., C290

MAFEKING RELIEVED, A8, C224

MAIDEN NAME, A6, B3, F1, F7, K12, K13, L3, App. 84

Mais, S. P. B., A3a

MAKE ME A PALATE, A8, C147

MAKING THE MOST OF THE BIG BAND, C351

MAN FROM DEFIANCE (OHIO), THE, A8, C289

MAN WHO NOTICED THINGS, A, F14, G19

Manchester Guardian, C57, C66, C71, C73, C79, C80, C90–3, C96–101, C111, L28, for later entries *see* *Guardian*

Mandrake, C28

Mansell Information Publishing Ltd., B14

Mantle in grey, the dusk steals slowly in, C7

Maples, Ann, A3b

Marrying left your maiden name disused, A6, B3, F1, F7, K12, K13, L3, App. 84

Marsh, P., A3b

Martin, Graham, G28, H10

Martz, Louis, A7b

Marvell Press, The, A6, F1, F3, H5

Marx, Erica, L2

MASTERS' VOICES, C167

May, Derwent, A10a

MAY WEATHER, C22

Meanjin quarterly, H4

Mellers, Wilfred, A8a

Mellor, Oscar, A5

Melly, George, A7a, A8a, C257

Melody Maker, C244

MEMORIES OF FESTIVALS PAST, A8, C239

Merwin, W. S., C66

Meryman, R., C393

Mezzrow, Mezz., C76

Michigan Quarterly Review, C382

Middleton, R., C414

MIGHTY MEZZ, THE, C76

MILES WITHOUT END, A8, C213

Millay, Edna St. Vincent, C73

Miller, Karl, F1

Millgate, M., C381

Milligan, I., App. 64

Mingus, C., C388

MINGUS=DUKE MINUS, A8, C234

MINGUS, MINGUS ETC., A8, C234

MISS BESSIE TO YOU, C376

MISS RIDLER AND MISS MILLAY, C73, L28

MISSING CHAIRS, C149

MR BLEANEY, A7, C51, C68, F2, F3, F7, F10, G11, G16, K13, L4, L14

MR POWELL'S MURAL, C375

Mitchell, Donald, A8a

Moat, John, L23

Modern Language Review, C86, C102

MODESTIES, A4, C94, C221, L21

MONEY, A10, F6

MONK [IN THE DAYLIGHT], A8, C225

Montgomery, Bruce, A1, A3, *see also* Crispin, Edmund

Month ago in fields, A, C22

Moon, Eric, A2c

Moon is full tonight, The, A1, B2

Moore, Geoffrey, App. 22

MORE TOADS RE-VISITED, C359

Morning, a glass door, flashes, A4

Morning has spread again, A1, B2, K5

Morning Telegraph [Sheffield], C283

Morrell, R., C270

Morris, Mervyn, H*n*

Morrison, Blake, App. 65

Morse, Samuel French, A6a

Mortimer, A. R., L9

Mortimer, J., A2d, A3d

MOULDIE FIGGES, C96

Mowbray, A. R. & Co., B1

MRS HARDY'S MEMORIES C171

Muir, Edwin, C124

Murphy, Richard, A10b, App. 66

MUSIC TO STAND UP TO, C342

MUST WE SWALLOW THE NEW WAVE?, A8, C264

My age fallen away like white swaddling, A6, C43, F1, F7, K5

MY BEST RECORD OF 1964, A8, C219

MY FIRST NAME IS JAMES, A8, C294

My sleep is made cold, A1, C110, K5

My wife and I have asked a crowd of craps, A10, C383, F6

MYTHOLOGICAL INTRODUCTION, B1, C27

MYXOMATOSIS, A6, C45, F1, K9, App. 70

Naremore, James, App. 67
Nash, Ogden, C149
National Theatre, H*n*
NATURALLY THE FOUNDATION
WILL BEAR YOUR EXPENSES, A7,
C143, C229, F3
NEGROES OF EUROPE, C414
NEW BUILDING, THE, D18
New Humanist, C404
New lines—II, L17
NEW ORLEANS PRESERV'D, A8,
C227
New Poems, 1955, L2
New Poems, 1956, L4
New Poems, 1957, L5
New Poems, 1958, B4
New Poems, 1961, L11
New Poems, 1962, L15
New Poems, 1970–71, L27
New Poems, 1975, L32
New Poetry, 1964, L19
New Review, The, C445, E19
NEW RUSSELL, THE, A8, C230
New Statesman, C33, C149, C155,
C167, C182, C209, C310, C312,
C313, C334, C353, C375, C383,
C402, C405, C427, C436, C440, H5
NEW WAVE SMOOTHED OUT, THE,
A8, C264
New World Writing, C68
New York Review of Books, C241,
F3
NEW YORKER BEAT, THE, C306
Newton, F., C107, C111
Newton, J. M., A7a
NEXT, PLEASE, A4, A6, B3, C48, F1,
F5, F7, K13, App. 9
Next year we are to bring the soldiers
home, A10, C329, F6
Nichols, Peter, L25
NIGHT-MUSIC, A1, K13
MCMXIV, A7, B13, C131, C150, F3,
K13, L20

No, I have never found, A6, C47, F1,
F7, K7, K13
NO MORE FEVER, C60
NO ROAD, A4, A6, C50, F1, F7,
L18, L22
Noel, John, App. 58
Norris, Leslie, B8
NORTH SHIP, THE, A1, K5, K10
NOSTALGIA CORNER, A8, C311
NOT AS WILD AS HIS NAME, A8,
C289
NOT LITERARY ENOUGH, C40
NOT MUCH DOING, MAN, C377
NOT THE PLACE'S FAULT, C104
NOTHING TO BE SAID, A7, C165,
F3, F4
Nott, Kathleen, C66, L5
Now night perfumes lie upon the air,
C9
NURSERY TALE, A1
Nye, Robert, A10a

Oakes, Philip, E8
Obedient daily dress, A6, B3, F1, F7,
L3
Oberg, Arthur, App. 68
OBSERVATION, C24
Observer, C107, C120, C181, C189,
C275, C397, C399, C400, C406,
C428, C437, C446, C449
O'Connor, William Van, L24, App.
23, App. 69
ODYSSEY FOR OLD-TIMERS, A8,
C236
Oh, no one can deny, A7, F3, K5
OILS, A4
OLD FOOLS, THE, A10, C416, F6
OLD HANDS IN NEW SLEEVES, A8,
C172
OLD MAN MAINSTREAM, A8, C295
Oliva, Renato, K10
Oliver, Douglas, E15
Oliver, P., C120, C248, C318, C340

On longer evenings, A4, A6, F1, F4, F7, K2, K5, L1, App. 50

On pillow after pillow lies, C404

On shallow slates the pigeons shift together, C70, G7

On shallow straw, in shadeless glass, A7, C215, F3, K13, L22

On the day of the explosion, A9, A10, C410, F6

ON THE WING, C208

Once I am sure there's nothing going on, A6, C56, F1, F7, G18, K1, K11, K13, K16, L3, L12, L22, App. 21, App. 26, App. 71, App. 84

One man walking a deserted platform, A1

Only in books the flat and final happens, C24

ONWARDS AND DOWNWARDS, C364

Open University, G27, G28, H10, App. 2

Opie, Iona and Peter, C112

Oppel, Horst, App. 21

ORNETTE AGAIN, A8, C288

Orr, Peter, F4, F6, F12

OUT OF THE HUSTLE, A8, C222

Overlook Press, The, A2e, A3e

Owen, Wilfred, C212, C439

OXFORD BOOK OF TWENTIETH-CENTURY VERSE, THE, B12, C417–421, F17, G24

Oxford Poetry, 1942–1943, B1

Oxford University Labour Club Bulletin, C24, C25

Oxford University Poetry Society, A5

P.E.N., B4, L11, L15, L27, L32

Packer, L. M., C226

Page, Norman, App. 70

PALGRAVE'S LAST ANTHOLOGY, C386

PANASSIÉ IN NEW ORLEANS, A8, C297

PANASSIÉ SIDES, THE, A8, C297

PANASSIÉ STOMPS, A8, C146

Paris Review, C88

Parker, Derek, A7a

PARKER LEGEND, THE, A8, C246

Parkinson, R. N., App. 71

PARTING IS SUCH SWEET SORROW, C5

Partisan Review, C229

PAST AND FUTURE FREEDOMS, A8, C302

Penguin Book of Contemporary Verse, The, L12

Pennati, Camillo, K10

Perry Jackson Grammar School, C186

PERSISTENCE OF THE BLUES, THE, A8, C140

Peschmann, Hermann, App. 72

Phoenix, C23, App. 4

PIANISTS NOT FOR SHOOTING, A8, C204

Pickrel, P., A3b

PIECES OF STRING, A8, C206

PIGEONS, C70, G7

PLACES, LOVED ONES, A6, C47, F1, F7, K7, K13

Planted deeper than roots, B1

Plater, Alan, Hn

Platform, C52

PLAYIN' MY SAXOPHONE, A8, C197

PLEASURE PRINCIPLE, THE, C83

Plomer, William, C128, L11

Plomley, Roy, G26

PLYMOUTH, C28

Poem-of-the-Month-Club, A9

POET ON THE 8.15, A, E7

Poet Speaks, The, record 8, F4

Poetry and Audience, C37, C40, C41, C69, L9

Poetry and Drama Magazine, C89

POETRY AT PRESENT, C78

POETRY BEYOND A JOKE, C99
Poetry Book Society, A7, B4, B16
Poetry Book Society Bulletin, C62, C221
Poetry Dimension, L30, L31
Poetry from Oxford in Wartime, B2
Poetry in the Making, B7
Poetry 1960, B5
Poetry 1967, L20
Poetry 1972, L29
Poetry Northwest, C110
POETRY OF DEPARTURES, A6, C41,
   C46, F1, F7, G12, K13, K14, K15,
   L9, L14
POETRY OF WILLIAM BARNES, THE,
   C178
Poetry Review, C150
Poetry Supplement, B16
Poet's Choice, B6
Poet's Eye, C280
POETS IN A FINE FRENZY AND
   OTHERWISE, C332
Poets of the 1950's, B3
PORTRAIT, C28
Poss, S., A10b
POSTERITY, A10, C313, F6
POST-HOLIDAY RECUPERATION,
   A8, C147
Pound, Ezra, C73, L28
Pour away that youth, A1, K13
Powell, Anthony, A3a, C32, C375
PRELUSIVE POEMS, C250
Press, John, A1c, C83, C97, C114,
   App. 73
Pritchard, W. H., A10b
Private Eye, B10
Private Library, A5
PROLOGUE, A10, B10, C406
PROSPECT BEHIND US, THE, A8,
   C195
Pryce-Jones, Alan, C115
PSYCHOLOGY AND VIVISECTION,
   C33
PUDDLETOWN MARTYR, THE, C440

Punch, C412
PURIST OF A SORT, A8, C285
Purnell & Sons, A3a
PUTTING THE MODERNS IN THEIR
   PLACE, A8, C146

Q, C32, C53, C54
Quaritch, Bernard, Ltd., J4
Quarterly, is it, money reproaches me,
   A10, F6
Queen, C268, E9
Queen's University, Belfast, C32,
   C53, C54
QUESTION OF ENVIRONMENT, A,
   C396
QUIET SNOOZE, A, C3

Raban, Jonathan, A7a
RABBIT JUMPS THE BLUES, A8, C326
RACIAL ART, A, C120
Radio Australia, F13, G20
Radio Times, C31, G13, G29
Rain patters on a sea that tilts and
   sighs, A6, B6, F1, F7
Raine, Kathleen, C57
Ramsey, F., Jr. *and* Smith, C. E., C81
Random House, A7b, c
RANGING THROUGH THE DECADES,
   A8, C172
READERS' GUIDE, D22, D24
Readers Union Arts Book Society,
   B12
READING HABITS [letter], C29
REAL COOL ALLEY, A8, C191
REAL MUSICIANER, A, C122
REAL WILFRED, C439
REASONS FOR ATTENDANCE, A6,
   F1, G5, K9, L2
Recognitions, C394
RECORD-MAKING HISTORY, C337
RECORDS OF THE YEAR, C192, C218,
   C240, C260, C282, C300, C327,
   C347, C373

Redgrove, Peter, C118
Redwood Burn Ltd., A6c
REFERENCE BACK, A7, C55, C88, F3, F7, L4, App. 84
REFERRED BACK, A7, C55, C88, F3, F7, L4, App. 84
REFLECTIONS AT CHRISTMASTIDE, C2
Reid, J. C., C117
Reisner, R. H., C208
REPORTS ON EXPERIENCE, C92
REQUIEM FOR JAZZ, C247
Review, The, C196, C359, C408
Review of English Studies, C386
REVIVAL THAT CAME TOO LATE, A, C338
Ricks, Christopher, A1c, A7b, C334, F3, App. 74
Ridler, Anne, A6a, C73, C113
Rigal, Denis, App. 94
Roberts, John, Ltd. *see* John Roberts Press Ltd.
Robinson, James K., App. 75
Robinson, M., App. 95
Robson, Jeremy, L30
Roe, H. E. A., C11, C15, C16
Rogers, Timothy, J4
Roper, Derek, App. 76
ROSE-RED-LIGHT CITY, A8, C162
Rosencrantz, T., C231
Rosenthal, M. L., A6b, App. 24, App. 25
Ross, Alan, C92, J7
Rossetti, Christina, C226
Rowe, Christopher *and* Clark, Ian, L26
Rowland, J. R., H4
Royal National Institute for the Blind, B12
Royal Society of Arts, C444
RUMMAGERS, THE, C336
Russell, Charles *pseud.* of Philip Larkin, C30

Russell, R., C423
Rust, Brian, C90, C266

SAD STEPS, A10, C313, F6, K2, K8
Sadleir, Michael, A3a
Sager, K., App. 26
St. Martin's Press, A2c, A3b, A6b, A8b
Sanesi, Roberto, K9
SATCHMO STILL, C393
Saturday Book, C131
Scannell, Vernon, C83, C118, F14, L15
School of Oriental and African Studies Library, B14
Scupham, Peter, B12
SELF'S THE MAN, A7, F3, K5
SEND NO MONEY, A7, B13, C189, F3, L17
Sense and Sensibility in Twentieth Century Writing, L24
70° N, A1, K5
75° N, A1, K5
Sexual intercourse began, A10, C301, C348, C362, F6
Seydi, Sevin, J1
Seymour-Smith, Martin, A1c, A7a
Shakespeare-Preis, 1976, B18, K6
SHAKESPEARE, THOU ART TRANS-LATED, A8, C232
Shanks, Edward, A3a
Shapiro, H., A6b
She kept her songs, they took so little space, A7, B5, F3, K5, K13, L10, L17, App. 74
SHEM THE PENMAN, C63
Shenandoah, C51, C161
Shoosmith, H., A6a
SHOULD JAZZ BE AN ART?, C181
SHOUT IT, MOAN IT, A8, C237
SHOUTING V. MOANING, A8, C237
SHOW SATURDAY, A10, C431, F6

Side by side, their faces blurred, A7, C58, C69, C75, F2, F3, F7, G7, K13, L5, L6, L9, L16

SIDNEY BECHET FROM NEW ORLEANS, A8, C251

Silkin, Jon, A6a, App. 80

Since the majority of me, A4, L1

Since we agreed to let the road between us, A4, A6, C50, F1, F7, L18, L22

Sinclair, J. McH., App. 27

Sissman, L. E., B12

Sito, Jerzy S., K12

65° N, A1, C110, K5

Skeat, T. C., B7

SKIN, A6, B3, F1, F7, L3

Slowly the women file to where he stands, A7, C130, C161, F3, K13, L11

Smith, F. G., C12

Smith, Martin Seymour-, *see* Seymour-Smith, Martin

Smith, Stevie, B15, C182, C399, H5

Smith, W., C248

SNAIL RACE VOLUNTARY, A8, C213

Snow, C. P. *Lord*, B12

SO FAST IS SO HIGH, A8, C249

So through that unripe day you bore your head, A1, B2, F5

Sola Buil, Ricardo, App. 96

SOLAR, A10, C268, F6, K8

Soljan, Antun, K15

SOME JAZZ BOOKS, C105

Some must employ the scythe, A4

SOME TENORS, A8, C245

Something to offer, L21

Sometimes you hear, fifth-hand, A6, C41, C46, F1, F7, G12, K13, K14, K15, L9, L14

SONNET, C26

SOUL FOOD, C277

SOUNDS OF A VETERANS' RALLY, C396

SOUNDS OF YESTERDAY, C380

Southerington, F. R., C381

Speaking of Writing, XIII, E4

Spectator, C34, C38, C39, C43–5, C47, C56, C112, C115, C117, C123, C126, C129, C135, C183, C187, C190, C198, C231, C273, C292, C352, F1

Spector, R. D., A7b

SPELL OF BASIN STREET, THE, A8, C162

Spellman, A. B., C292

Spender, Stephen, B12, L4, App. 77

Sprigge, E., C71

SPRING, A4, A6, F1, K5, K9

SPRING WARNING, C17

Springtime [one], L1

SQUALOR BEHIND THE BLUES, C341

Squire, Sir John Collings, C115

Stafford, William, A7b

Stallworthy, Jon, C428, C439, L27

Standard of Verse, A, L23

Standing under the fobbed belly, A7, B13, C189, F3, L17

Stands the Spring!—heralded by its bright-clothed, C7

Stearns, M., C84

Stein, Gertrude, C71

STEVIE, GOOD-BYE, C399

Stiftung F. V. S., Hamburg, B18, K6

Stock, Noel, App. 78

Stockwell, Robert, Ltd., B11

Stojiljković, Vlada, K14

STONE CHURCH DAMAGED BY A BOMB, A, B1

Stonesifer, R., C201

Stoppard, Tom, B11

Stopping the diary, A10, F6

STORY, C20

Stow, Randolph, C108

STRAIGHT AND TRUE, A8, C256

Strange to know nothing, never to be sure, A7, C61, F3

Stratford, Jenny, B7, B15, I1

STREET LAMPS, C14

Stubbs, John Heath- *see* Heath-Stubbs, John

Studley Press, Inc., The, A2e, A3e

STUDY OF READING HABITS, A, A7, C133, F3, K5, L17, L21

SUCCESS STORY, C72, C85, App. 62

Suddenly clouds of snow, A1, K5

Sudhalter, R. *and* Evans, P. R., C436

Summer is fading, A7, C121, F3, K4

SUMMER NOCTURNE, C9

Sun. Tree. Beginning. God in a thicket. Crown., A4

Sunday Telegraph, C411

Sunday Times, C163, C329, C447, E8

SUNNY PRESTATYN, A7, C194, F3

SUPERLATIVELY ALONE, C293

SUPPORTING GROUPS MAKE HISTORY, C360

SUPREME SOPHISTICATES, C412

SURNAME UNADORNED, C304, C305

SURVIVAL OF THE HOTTEST, A8, C151

Suspended lion face, A10, C268, F6, K8

Sutton, James Ballard, A1, A2

Swerving east, from rich industrial shadows, A7, C155, F3, F5, H10, H16, K4, K13, L23, L26

Swinden, Patrick, App. 79

SWINGING ANCIENT AND MODERN, C345

SYMPATHY IN WHITE MAJOR, A10, C298, F6

Szabó, Lőrinc, K7

TAKE ONE HOME FOR THE KIDDIES, A7, C215, F3, K13, L22

TALKING IN BED, A7, C134, F3, K5

TASTE OF THE PAST, C349

Taylor, Geoffrey, A6a

Taylor, R., C106

Tempo, C200

TENDER VOICES, C193

Tennyson, Alfred, *Lord*, C334

TENOR PLAYER WITH 50 LEGS, THE, A8, C252

TESTIFYIN' TO THE BLUES TRADITION, C248

Texas Quarterly, C134

THAT EDWARDIAN RAG, A8, C224

THAT NICE BOY, C436

That note you hold, narrowing and rising, shakes, A7, C67, C180, F3, K5, K13, L17

That was a pretty one, I heard you call, A7, C55, C88, F3, F7, L4, App. 84

That Whitsun, I was late getting away, A7, C109, F3, F5, F15, G22, K5, K13, L8, L12, L14, L17, L22, App. 41, App. 64

There is an evening coming in, A4, A6, B3, C394, F1, F7, K2, K4, K5, L14, L21

They fuck you up, your mum and dad, A10, F6, K8

THEY'LL NONE OF THEM BE MISSED, A8, C242

THIS BE THE VERSE, A10, F6, K8

This empty street, this sky to blandness scoured, A6, C37, C39, F1, F7, L3

This is the first thing, A1, K5

This town has docks where channel boats come sidling, A5, A6, C53, F1, F7, K5, K13

This was Mr Bleaney's room. He stayed, A7, C51, C68, F2, F3, F7, F10, G11, G16, K13, L4, L14

This was your place of birth, this daytime palace, A1, C26, K13

Thomas, R. S., C92

Those long uneven lines, A7, B13, C131, C150, F3, K13, L20

"Thou was not born for death, immortal bird, C8
THREE-TENOR FIGHT, A8, C207
THUNDERING HERDS [OF WOODY HERMAN], A8, C211
Thurley, Geoffrey, App. 28
Thwaite, Anthony, B15, C419, F2, F10, F17, G11, G24, L11, App. 29–31, App. 80
Tightly-folded bud, A6, C44, F1, L3
TIMBRES VARIED, C231
Time running beneath the pillow wakes, C25
Times, The, C304, C305, C355, C357, C398, C409, C435, C438, E4
Times Educational Supplement, C64, E1, E13
Times Higher Education Supplement, C425, E17, H15
Times Literary Supplement, C95, C144, C169, C254, C308, C317, C325, C377, C407, C415, C417, C420, C430, C441
TIMES, PLACES, LOVED ONES, A6, C47
Timms, David, App. 5
Tired of a landscape known too well when young, C20
To fail (transitive and intransitive), C72, C85, App. 62
To step over the low wall that divides, A10, C348, C429, F6, K13, L27
TO THE SEA, A10, C348, C429, F6, K13, L27
To wake, and hear a cock, A1
To write one song, I said, A1, K5, K13
TOADS, A6, C42, F1, F7, L3, L14, L21
TOADS REVISITED, A7, C190, C241, F3, L19
Tobin, J., A6b
Tomlinson, Charles, App. 81

TOPS, C74, G7
Tops heel and yaw, C74, G7
Torch, C75, C105, C193, C250, C265, C361
Torchlight, C125, C184, C262, C330, C395, E2, E3, E6, E11
Tracks, A2a, E10
TREES, THE, A10, C310, C391, C429, F6, K8
Trees are coming into leaf, The, A10, C310, C391, C429, F6, K8
TRIAL OF FAITH, C370
TRIPLE TIME, A6, C37, C39, F1, F7, L3
TRUMPET PRELIMINARY, A8, C153
Trumpet's voice, loud and authoritative, The, A6, F1, G5, K9, L2
Truth, C76, C81, C84
Turret Books, B7, B15
TWENTIES SWAN SONG, A8, C255
Twentieth Century, C143
Twentieth Century Love Poems, L18
XX POEMS, A4, App. 49
TWILIGHT OF TWO [THE] OLD GODS, A8, C319
TWO PORTRAITS OF SEX, A4
TWO SIDES TO HODGES, A8, C326

UGLY SISTER, A1
Ulanov, B., C91
ULTIMATUM, C19
UNACKNOWLEDGED LEGISLATORS, C340
Umbrella, C104
United Nations Conference on the Human Environment, 1972, B10
University College, Leicester, C30, C434
University of Durham Institute of Education, C72
University of Hull, C75, C105, C125, C185, C193, C320, C359, C361, C365, C378, C389, C395, D passim,

University of Hull—(*contd.*)
E2, E3, E6, E11, E18, F3, F4–6,
F10, H6, H16

University of Hull Bulletin, C442,
C443

University of Hull Gazette, C320,
C365, C378, C389, C426

*University of Leicester Convocation
Review*, C434

University of London, School of
Oriental and African Studies, *see*
School of Oriental and African
Studies

University of St. Andrews, H12

University of York, E12

UNIVERSITY'S LIBRARY, THE, D15,
D19, D27

UNNATURAL BREAKS, A8, C242

UNSUNG GOLD MEDALLIST, THE,
E8

Unwin Brothers Ltd., B4

UP FROM THE SOUTH, A8, C175

Ure, Peter, App. 82

Vajdá, Miklos, K7

Van Deel, T., K2

VENUTI AND LANG, A8, C206

VERNON WATKINS: AN ENCOUN-
TER AND A RE-ENCOUNTER,
B8, C335, K17

Vernon Watkins, 1906–1967, B8

VERS DE SOCIÉTÉ, A10, C383, F6

Verstegen, Peter, K2

Vetter, Edgar A., F2

Villiers Publications, A6a, B7, B15

VINTAGE YEARS, THE, A8, C299

VOICES AS INSTRUMENTS, C382

VOICES FROM THE SOUTH, A8,
C175

Wagstaff, M., C186

Wain, John, A8a, A10a, C177, H*n*,
App. 32, App. 83, App. 84

Waiting for breakfast, while she
brushed her hair, A1c–d, A4, C62

Wakeman, John, H14

Walker, Peter, B10

Walking around in the park, A7,
C190, C241, F3, L19

WANDERING MINSTRELS, A8, C222

WANTED: GOOD HARDY CRITIC,
C270

WANTS, A4, A6, C163, C394, F1, F4,
F7, K1, K4, K13, L1, L14

WAR POET, THE, C212

Warburg, J., C102

Watching the shied core, A7, C137,
C216, F3

WATER, A7, C82, C89, C394, F3, L17

Watkins, Vernon, B8, C113, C335,
K18

Watson, J. R., App. 85

Wave, C366

WAY DOWN YONDER, A8, C236

WAY OUT IN ALL DIRECTIONS, A8,
C252

WE PROTEST, C11

Weatherhead, A. K., App. 86

Weber, Brom, L24

WEDDING-WIND, A4, A6, B3, C394,
F1, F5, L1, L14, App. 9, App. 26

Weekend Telegraph, C247

Weiss, Theodore, App. 87

Welland-Freeman, Ruth, K3

Wellington Public Library, H1

Welz, Dieter, App. 33, App. 88

Wesling, Donald, App. 89

Western Printing Services, B13

What are days for?, A7, C82, C89,
C394, F3, F4, F5, G18, K5

What do they think has happened, the
old fools, A10, C416, F6

WHATEVER HAPPENED?, A5, A6,
F1, K7

WHEN BLUES ARE TAKEN AS READ,
C333

When getting my nose in a book, A7, C133, F3, K5, L17, L21

When I drop four cubes of ice, A10, C298, F6

When I see a couple of kids, A10, F6

When I throw back my head and howl, B16, L32

When night slinks, like a puma, down the sky, C14

WHEN ROCKER GOES MOD, A8, C230

When the Russian tanks roll westward, H7

WHEN THEY STILL MADE NICE NOISES, A8, C322

WHERE EUROPE IS UNRIVALLED, C369

White, Josh, C238

White girl lay on the grass, A, B1, C27

WHITE-HOT BLUES, A8, C303

WHITE WORLD, THE, A8, C136

Whitstable Litho Straker Brothers Ltd., A1d, A2d, A3d

WHITSUN WEDDINGS, THE, A7, C109, F3, F5, F15, G22, K5, K10, K13, L8, L12, L14, L17, L22, App. 41, App. 64

Who called love conquering, A4

WHOSE FLAMING YOUTH?, A8, C311

Why should I let the toad work, A6, C42, F1, F7, L3, L14, L21

Widest prairies have electric fences, The A4, A6, C34, F1

Wilbur, Richard, C79

WILD OATS, A7, C196, F3, K5

Willetts, R. F., K1

Williamson, K., C122

Wind blew all my wedding-day, The, A4, A6, B3, C394, F1, F5, L1, L14, App. 9, App. 26

WINTER, A1, C394, K5, K13

WINTER NOCTURNE, C7

WIRES, A4, A6, C34, F1

Wiseman, Christopher, App. 90

Within the dream you said, A1, K5, K13

WITHOUT THE DUKE, A8, C168

Wolpe, Margaret, A3a

"A woman has ten claws, A1, K5

Words as plain as hen-birds' wings, A4, C94, C221, L21

Wright, David, A6a

WRITER, A, C21

York, University see University of York

YOU DO SOMETHING FIRST, C71

"You will go a long journey, A1, K5

Young, K., A6a

YOUNG REVOLUTIONARIES, A8, C170

'YOU'RE A GENIUS', A8, C176